Also see:
Array, Symbol

(hash, pound or number sign) is used to prefix a literal symbol or array.

```
#address          "a literal symbol"
#( 1 2 3 4)       "a literal array of 4 integers"
```

Also see:
Character

$

$ (dollar sign) is used to prefix a literal character.

```
$A                "a literal character A represented by ASCII
                  hexadecimal code 0041"
$$                "a literal character $ represented by ASCII
                  hexadecimal code 0024"
```

Also see:
Expressions

.

. (full stop) is used as a statement separator.

In the following expression series, no full stop is required after the final statement because it is a statement separator NOT a statement terminator. The variable declaration |a b sum| is not classed as a statement, hence no full stop.

```
|a b sum|
a := 4.
b:= 5.
sum := a + b
```

Also see:
Arguments, Block, Keyword message

: (colon) is used to prefix a block parameter. See *Block*.

A colon is also used to suffix keywords in keyword message selectors to show where an argument follows.

The following message expression contains the keyword message selector; `credit:`.

    myAccount credit: 250

In the next expression, the keyword message selector is `transfer: to:`.

    myAccount transfer: 350 to: yourAccount

Also see:
Expressions

; (semi-colon) is used to cascade message sequences. It provides a shorthand way of writing a sequence of messages that are all being sent to the same receiver.

Also see:
Assignment

:= (colon followed by equals sign) is an assignment operator.

An assignment is used to make a variable refer to an object.

In the following statement, the variable `age` is made to reference the integer object 18.

    `age := 18`

The `:=` sign can be read as *refers to*. Therefore, in this case, `age` re*fers to* 18.

Also see:
Answer

^

---

^ (caret) is used as an answer marker. It prefixes the expression that is used to produce the answer returned when a message is sent to an object.

For example, assuming we have a class **Person** with attribute `age`, the *getter* method `age` could be used to return the value of `age`.

    `age`
        `"Getter method to answer the value of the age attribute of the receiver"`

        `^ age`

If `aPerson` is an instance of class **Person** and the object referenced by the instance variable `age` is `18`, then the following message expression answers 18.

    `aPerson age`

If a method contains more than one answer expression, the first to be evaluated returns its value and causes the method execution to end.

In the following message expression, the boolean object `true` is returned as the answer if the condition `(age=18)` evaluates to `true`, otherwise the answer given is `false`.

    `(age = 18)`
        `ifTrue:  [^true]`
        `ifFalse: [^false]`

,

Also see:
Concatenate, String

, (comma) is a binary message selector used for concatenating or joining together two instances of **SequenceableCollection**. This includes instances of **Array, ByteString, Symbol, OrderedCollection** and **SortedCollection**.

In the following expression, two **ByteString** objects are concatenated.

    'Small' , 'talk'

'Small' is the receiver and 'talk' is the argument.
The message , 'talk' is sent to the receiver, answering 'Smalltalk'.

concatenate: is a keyword message selector that is used specifically for concatenating strings.
In the expression;

    'milk' concatenate: 'shake'

'milk' is the receiver and 'shake' is the argument.
The message concatenate: 'shake' is sent to the receiver, answering 'milkshake'.

+

Also see:
Arithmetic operators

+ (plus sign) is a binary message selector used for arithmetic addition.
Its receiver and its argument must be arithmetic values.

In the following expression, 3 is the receiver and 5 is the argument.

    3 + 5

The message +5 is sent to the receiver, answering 8.

`plus:` is a keyword message selector that is also used for arithmetic addition.

In the next expression, `4` is the receiver and `9` is the argument.

    `4 plus: 9`

The message `plus:9` is sent to the receiver, answering `13`.

Also see:
Arithmetic operators   -

`-` (minus sign) is a binary message selector used for arithmetic subtraction. Its receiver and its argument must be arithmetic values.

In the following expression, `8` is the receiver and `5` is the argument.

    `8 - 5`

The message `-5` is sent to the receiver, answering `3`.

Also see:
Arithmetic operators   *

`*` (asterisk) is a binary message selector used for arithmetic multiplication. Its receiver and its argument must be arithmetic values.

In the following expression, `3` is the receiver and `2` is the argument.

    `3 * 2`

The message `*2` is sent to the receiver, answering `6`.

> Also see:
> **Arithmetic operators**

/

/ (forward slash) is a binary message selector used for arithmetic division. Its receiver and its argument must be arithmetic values.

In the following expression, 8 is the receiver and 4 is the argument.

    8 / 4

The message /4 is sent to the receiver, answering 2.

If one integer instance does not divide exactly into the other, the result is a rational number, and is expressed as a fraction.

The following expression answers (7/3), an instance of the class **Fraction**.

    7 / 3

When an instance of **Float** is divided by another instance of **Float**, the answer is also an instance of **Float**.

Therefore the following expression answers 1.75.

    7.0 / 4.0

> Also see:
> **Arithmetic operators**

**

** (double asterisk) is a binary message selector used to raise the receiver to the power of the argument. Its receiver and its argument must be arithmetic values.

The following expression answers the value 4^2, ie 16.

    4 ** 2

Also see:
Arithmetic operators

//

// (double forward slash) is a binary message selector used for integer division. Its receiver and its argument must be arithmetic values.

The following expression answers `1`.

        7.0 // 4.0

The message selector **//** always produces an integer result, truncating the decimal part.

Note that if the result is negative, then **//** division truncates toward negative infinity, therefore the following expression answers `-2`.

        7.0 // -4.0

Also see:
Arithmetic operators

\\

**** (double backward slash) is a binary message selector used for obtaining the remainder from integer division, after which the sign of the answer is set to be the same as that of the argument.

The following expression answers `1`. This is because `9` divided by `4` equals `2` with a remainder `1`.

        9 \\ 4

In the next expression the argument is negative.

        9 \\ -4

When we divide `9` by `-4` the real answer is `-2.25`. However, integer division truncates the result down to the nearest integer, which in this case will be `-3`. (Remember that `-2` is higher in value than `-2.25`.) We would

expect a division by -4 to give the answer -3 if the numerator is 12. In the example expression it is 9, thus integer division gives the absolute remainder as 3. The sign of the argument (ie -4) is negative, therefore the answer returned is -3.
The following expression answers 3.

```
-9 \\ 4
```

And the next answers -1.

```
-9 \\ -4
```

> &

Also see:
Boolean, Logical operators

`&` (ampersand) is a binary message selector representing logical **and**.

Boolean expressions (ie expressions that evaluate to `true` or `false`) can be combined to give a single logical result.

The message format is;
    boolean expression & *boolean expression*

The `&` message selector compares its receiver and argument, returning `true` if both are `true`, and `false` otherwise.

This can be represented in a truth table, which shows all possible values of receiver and argument, with the corresponding answers.

Receiver	Argument	& answer
false	false	false
false	true	false
true	false	false
true	true	true

The following expression evaluates to `true` if age is 19 or 20, otherwise `false`.

```
(age > 18) & (age < 21)
```

8

(Note that the parentheses are required in the previous expression, otherwise problems will occur due to inappropriate order of evaluation.)

`and:` is a keyword selector that behaves in a similar way to `&`.

The format for use is;
 boolean expression `and:` [*boolean expression*]

The receiver must evaluate to `true` or `false`, as must the code block within the square brackets.
`and:` combines the two results to give a single boolean value.

The following evaluates to `true` if `age` is `19` or `20`, otherwise `false`.

 `(age > 18) and: [age < 21]`

Note that there is a difference in the way `&` and `and:` work. In the case of `and:`, the code in the block is not evaluated until after the boolean receiver has been found to be `true` or `false`. This constitutes a slight processing shortcut compared to `&`. However, use of `&` makes the code easier to read.

Also see:
 Block, Boolean, Logical operators,
 Temporary variable

|

`|` (vertical bar) is a binary message selector representing logical **or**.

Boolean expressions (ie expressions that evaluate to `true` or `false`) can be combined to give a single logical result.

The format for use is;
 boolean expression `|` *boolean expression*

The `|` message selector compares its receiver and argument, returning `true` if either are `true`, and `false` otherwise.

9

This can be represented in a truth table, which shows all possible values of receiver and argument with the corresponding answers.

Receiver	Argument	answer
false	false	false
false	true	true
true	false	true
true	true	true

The following evaluates to `true` if `age` is under `18`, or if `age` is over `21`, otherwise `false`.

```
(age < 18) | (age > 21)
```

(Note that the parentheses are required in the previous expression, otherwise problems will occur due to inappropriate order of evaluation.)

`or:` is a keyword selector that behaves in a similar way to `|`.

The format for use is;
> *boolean expression* `or:` [*boolean expression*]

The receiver must evaluate to `true` or `false`, as must the code block within the square brackets.
`or:` combines the two results to give a single boolean value.

The following evaluates to `true` if `age` is under `18`, or if `age` is over `21`, otherwise `false`.

```
(age < 18) or: [age > 21]
```

Note that there is a difference in the way `|` and `or:` work. In the case of `or:`, the code in the block is not evaluated until after the boolean receiver has been found to be `true` or `false`. This constitutes a slight processing shortcut compared to `|`. However, use of `|` makes the code easier to read.

The `|` symbol is also used to delimit temporary variable declarations, as in;
> `|myAccount yourAccount|`

It is also used to separate block parameters from the expressions inside blocks.

10

Also see:
Logical operators

==

== (double equals) is a binary message selector to test for sameness or identity.

The **==** message selector compares the identities of its receiver and argument, both of which can be any class of object, returning `true` if they are exactly the same object, and `false` otherwise.

Smalltalk allows 32-bit address pointers to reference objects. The test for identity checks whether the addresses of two object references show that they point to the same object.
Objects of class **Boolean**, **SmallInteger**, **Character** and **UndefinedObject** are stored using less than 32 bits so their values are held directly rather than using a reference pointer.

The following expression answers `false` because there are two copies of the string stored in different places, and the pointers are not the same address value, even though the string objects referenced happen to have the same value.

    'Eric' == 'Eric'

However, the next expression evaluates to `true` because the object 2 is not stored using a pointer and is therefore being compared with itself.

    2 == 2

The following expressions both answer `true`.

    nil == nil
    $A == $A

Also, because of the way they are stored, Symbols with the same name answer `true`. For example;

    #label == #label

Comparing two separate arrays will answer `false` even if their contents are identical. For example;

    #(3 4 5) == #(3 4 5)

11

~~

Also see:
Logical operators

~~ (double tilde) is a binary message selector, which checks that two object references are not to the same object. It returns `true` if both are not exactly the same object, and `false` otherwise.

The following expression evaluates to `false` because 2 and 2 are exactly the same object.

    2 ~~ 2

=

Also see:
Logical operators

= (equals sign) is a binary message selector, which compares the value of its receiver with that of its argument, answering `true` if the receiver is equal in value to the argument, and `false` otherwise.

The objects being compared must be comparable objects such as numbers, characters, strings or symbols.

The following expression evaluates to `false` because 4 is not equal in value to 2.

    4 = 2

The next expression evaluates to `true` because `'Eric'` is equal in value to `'Eric'`.

    'Eric' = 'Eric'

If we had a **Car** class with attributes `colour` and `make`, we might expect that;

    myCar = yourCar

would answer `true` if `myCar` and `yourCar` both represent Blue Volvos.

12

However, when we compare objects of our own classes using =, the implementation defined in the **Object** class will be inherited. Here's the method code.

```
= anObject
    "Answer whether the receiver and the argument
    represent the same object."
    ^self == anObject
```

As you can see, the method uses == to check whether the objects being compared are the same object.
Thus;

    myCar = yourCar

effectively becomes;

    myCar == yourCar

and will only return true if they are actually the same object.

You can, of course, override the inherited = method with one of your own that compares each of the variable values.

Also see:
Logical operators

~=

~= (tilde followed by equals sign) is a binary message selector, which compares the value of its receiver with that of its argument, answering true if the receiver is not equal in value to the argument, and false otherwise.

The objects being compared must be comparable objects such as numbers, characters, strings or symbols.

The following expression evaluates to true because 4 is not equal in value to 2.

    4 ~= 2

The next expression evaluates to false because 'Eric' is equal in value to 'Eric'.

    'Eric' ~= 'Eric'

13

> <
>
> *Also see:*
> **Logical operators**

< (less than) is a binary message selector, which compares the value of its receiver with that of its argument, answering `true` if the receiver is less than the argument, and `false` otherwise.

The objects being compared must be comparable objects such as numbers, characters, strings or symbols.

The following expression evaluates to `false` because 4 is not less than 2.

        4 < 2

> <=
>
> *Also see:*
> **Logical operators**

<= (less than or equal to) is a binary message, which compares the value of its receiver with that of its argument, answering `true` if the receiver is less than or equal in value to the argument, and `false` otherwise.

The objects being compared must be comparable objects such as numbers, characters, strings or symbols.

The following expressions evaluate to `true` because 2 is equal in value to 2 (it is the same object), and 2 is less than 4.

        2 <= 2.
        2 <= 4

The next expression evaluates to `false` because 4 is not less than, or equal to 2.

        4 <= 2

Also see:
Logical operators

> **>**

> (greater than) is a binary message, which compares the value of its receiver with that of its argument, answering `true` if the receiver is greater than the argument, and `false` otherwise.

The objects being compared must be comparable objects such as numbers, characters, strings or symbols.

The following expression evaluates to `true` because 4 is greater than 2.

```
4 > 2
```

Also see:
Logical operators

> **>=**

>= (greater than or equal to) is a binary message, which compares the value of its receiver with that of its argument, answering `true` if the receiver is greater than or equal in value to the argument, and `false` otherwise.

The objects being compared must be comparable objects such as numbers, characters, strings or symbols.

The following expressions evaluate to `true` because 2 is equal in value to 2 (they are the same object), and 4 is greater than 2.

```
2 >= 2.
4 >= 2
```

The next expression evaluates to `false` because 2 is not greater than, or equal to, 4.

```
2 >= 4
```

15

> Also see:
> **Instance creation**

@ (at sign) is a binary message selector used to create instances of the class **Point**. **Point** objects are for producing two-dimensional graphics and refer to a position on two-dimensional axes. **Point** has two instance variables; the x coordinate (ie position relative to the horizontal axis) and the y coordinate (ie position relative to the vertical axis).

The expression;
```
4 @ 9
```

creates an instance of **Point** representing x, y coordinates (4,9).

Sending this point the message x, answers the x coordinate; 4.

```
(4 @ 9) x
```

and the y message answers the y coordinate; 9.

```
(4 @ 9) y
```

> Also see:
> **Association, Instance creation**

-> (minus followed by greater than sign) is a binary message selector used to create instances of class **Association**. An association is a *key-value* pair.

The expression;

```
anAssociation := (4 -> 'Eric')
```

creates a new instance of **Association** with the key set to 4 and the corresponding value set to the string 'Eric'.

16

Also see:
   Precedence

( )

( ) (parentheses) are used to enclose message expressions to clarify or alter the precedence. Precedence rules determine the priority order of evaluation.

Evaluation of expressions takes place starting with the expression inside the innermost parentheses.

In the statement;

```
(5 + (6 * (3 - 2)))
```

the expression `(3 - 2)` is evaluated first, resulting in;

```
(5 + (6 * 1))
```

`(6 * 1)` is evaluated next, giving;

```
(5 + 6)
```

which is evaluated to answer `11`.

Pairs of parentheses can be nested inside one another to any depth, although too many unnecessary parentheses make code harder to read, and increase the chance of making a mistake.

Remember that every open parenthesis must be matched by a corresponding close parenthesis. If you see one on its own, you can be sure it's up to no good!

[ ]

Also see:
Block

[ ] (square brackets) are used to enclose code blocks. Blocks are objects that are instances of class **BlockClosure**.

Evaluation of the expressions within a block is deferred, and is under the control of the Smalltalk environment at run time. Whereas other lines of program code are run in sequence, the code within a block is executed only if and when the required conditions are met.

For example, consider the message expression;

```
(age < 17)
    ifTrue:    [^'Under 17']
    ifFalse:   [^'Old enough to drive']
```

Here the blocks (enclosed in [ ]) are being used as message arguments. If the (age < 17) receiver evaluates to true, Smalltalk evaluates the ifTrue: argument block. However, if (age < 17) answers false, then the ifFalse: argument block is evaluated.

Smalltalk has to decide at run time which of the arguments to evaluate. It is not until run time that it knows the value referred to by age. Block objects are required so that evaluation is under Smalltalk's control.

Also see:
 Class, Inheritance

Abstract class

An abstract class is a class used to define the common attributes and behaviour of its subclasses. Other classes inherit from it but it can have no instances of its own.

For example, consider a university library system that uses a class named **Member**, which has instance variables; `membershipNumber`, `name` and `address`. If we assume that all library members are either staff or students of the university, we can make **Member** an abstract class, with **Staff** and **Student** its subclasses.

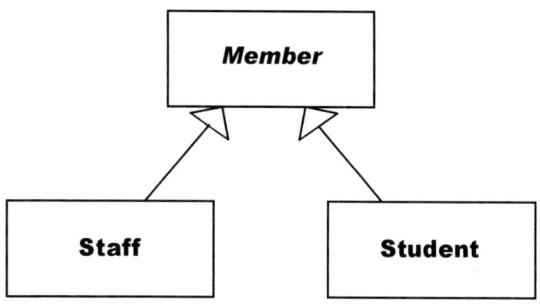

Instances of **Staff** and **Student** would inherit **Member** instance variables `membershipNumber`, `name` and `address`, but can also extend these with additional instance variables of their own. For example, **Staff** could have instance variable `roomNumber`, and **Student** could have a `courseName` instance variable. We would now never create an object that is just a member of the library; it is either an instance of **Staff** or an instance of **Student**. The **Member** class exists simply to provide the attributes and behaviour that are common to both **Staff** and **Student**.

Because we can create instances of **Staff** and of **Student**, these are said to be concrete classes. A concrete class is a class that can be used to create object instances. This term describes all classes that are not abstract classes.

The methods defined by a class control how the class and its instances can be accessed and used. In this way, methods define the protocol for communication with objects. Abstract classes define a common protocol for their subclasses through inheritance.

In our example, instances of class **Staff** would have instance variables;
`membershipNumber`	"inherited from **Member**"
`name`	"inherited from **Member**"
`address`	"inherited from **Member**"
`roomNumber`	"declared in **Staff**"

and will respond to messages;
`membershipNumber`	"getter method for `membershipNumber` inherited from **Member**"
`membershipNumber: aNumber`	"setter method for `membershipNumber` inherited from **Member**"
`name`	"getter method for `name` inherited from **Member**"
`name: aString`	"setter method for `name` inherited from **Member**"
`address`	"getter method for `address` inherited from **Member**"
`address: aString`	"setter method for `address` inherited from **Member**"
`roomNumber`	"getter method for `roomNumber` implemented in **Staff**"
`roomNumber: aNumber`	"setter method for `roomNumber` implemented in **Staff**"

Instances of class **Student** would have instance variables;
`membershipNumber`	"inherited from **Member**"
`name`	"inherited from **Member**"
`address`	"inherited from **Member**"
`courseName`	"declared in **Student**"

and will respond to messages;
`membershipNumber`	"getter method for `membershipNumber` inherited from **Member**"
`membershipNumber: aNumber`	"setter method for `membershipNumber` inherited from **Member**"
`name`	"getter method for `name` inherited from **Member**"
`name: aString`	"setter method for `name` inherited from **Member**"

`address`	"getter method for `address` inherited from **Member**"
`address: aString`	"setter method for `address` inherited from **Member**"
`courseName`	"getter method for `courseName` implemented in **Student**"
`courseName: aName`	"setter method for `courseName` implemented in **Student**"

In a sense, a Smalltalk class is never abstract because it is always possible to create instances. However, a class can be said to be abstract if an instance created from it will not function properly because at least one of its instance methods passes implementation responsibility to its subclasses.

To illustrate this, consider a **Shape** class for handling graphic objects. We'll make **Shape** an abstract class with subclasses **Ellipse** and **Rectangle**.

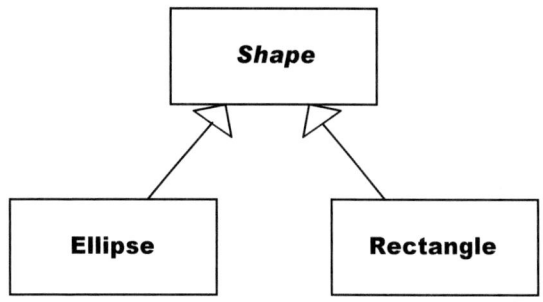

Class: **Shape**

Instance variables:

`topLeft`	"x, y coordinate position of top left corner of bounding box"
`bottomRight`	"x, y coordinate position of bottom right corner of bounding box"

Instance methods:

`topLeft: aPoint`	"setter method for `topLeft`"
`bottomRight: aPoint`	"setter method for `bottomRight`"
`draw`	"causes a shape to draw itself on screen"

The following diagram shows an instance of **Ellipse** with its bounding box.

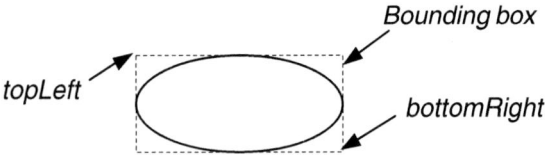

Although the **Shape** class specifies that the draw method must exist for shapes, its implementation is left to the subclasses of **Shape**. Hence, our concrete subclasses, **Ellipse** and **Rectangle**, will inherit the attributes and behaviour defined in **Shape**, but MUST implement their own methods called draw.

The draw method is implemented in the **Shape** class as follows;

> **draw**
> "Abstract method to draw a shape on the screen.
> Subclasses must override."
>   ^self subclassResponsibility

If the subclass fails to override this method, when an instance of the subclass is sent the message draw, it will cause this inherited method code to be executed, generating an exception and giving rise to an error message along the lines;

> 'My subclass should have overridden one of my messages'

Abstraction

Also see:
Object-oriented programming

Abstraction is a term used to describe the selective hiding of information not considered to be important to understanding the task in hand.

For example, if I use the word *aeroplane*, you will understand that I am referring to a flying vehicle with wings, without me filling in these details. This is a form of abstraction.

When developing software, we can use abstraction to simplify the problems we are trying to solve. Object-oriented programming lends itself particularly well to this principle.

If we were to design a system to handle theatre seat bookings, we might consider some abstractions, such as; *Seat* and *Performance*. We could list some possible attributes of these. Using *Seat* as an example, we could consider attributes;

>upholstery pattern
>seat number
>width
>price

But, of these, we might decide that only seat number and price are of interest to us. By describing *Seat* with just these relevant attributes, we simplify the concept to include only what is pertinent to us.

Also see:
Methods, Instance method

Accessor method

Accessor methods are used to set and get the values of instance variables. Individually they are sometimes called *setter methods* and *getter methods*. By convention these methods have the same name as the variables they affect.

Assuming we have a class **Person** that defines `age` as an instance variable, the following accessor methods could be provided to set and get `age`.

Setter method:
```
age : aNumber
"Sets the value of the age attribute.  Answers
the receiver"
    age := aNumber
```

Getter method:
```
age
"Answers the value of the age attribute"
    ^ age
```

Sending an instance of **Person** the message `age: 21` would set the value of its `age` variable to `21`. Sending the message `age` would answer the value of the age attribute.

23

Answer

Also see:
^ , Messages

When a message is sent to an object, it must give an answer, and the answer is always another object. If the method corresponding to the message defines no specific answer to be returned, the default answer will be the object that received the message.

Evaluation of the following expression returns the answer; 8.

```
5 + 3
```

Assuming that the next expression returns the default, the answer will be the object aPerson.

```
aPerson name: 'Eric'
```

Method names often give an indication of the class of the object that will be returned.
For example, the messages isEmpty and isNil return a **Boolean** object; true or false, and; asString returns a **String** object.

Within the implementation code for a method, the ^ prefix is used to denote the expression that is to provide the answer when the method finishes.

Because the default answer is the receiver object, there is no need to make the last line of a method;

```
^self        "returns the receiver"
```

However, sometimes it is useful to return self explicitly. In the following example, if the boolean condition evaluates to false, the method ends. If it is true, the method execution continues.

```
(boolean condition)
       ifFalse: [^self].
self something1.
self something2
```

24

Anthropomorphism

The term anthropomorphism describes the attributing of human qualities to things that are not human. This is sometimes a technique used by human-computer interface designers in an attempt to make the computer appear 'friendly' to the user.
For example, the kind of error message that says;
```
'My subclass should have overridden one of my
messages'
```

Some argue that it can be misleading and annoying to make computers appear to have a personality that they, of course, don't have. However, anthropomorphism often creeps into conversations about objected-oriented software.

For example;
> *'Who is this message sent to?'* (with *'who'* representing a software object)

or;
> *'These objects have display methods so they know how to draw themselves'*

Such language can help developers in thinking about the interactions between objects.

Also see:
Block, Methods

Arguments

Arguments are objects to be passed to a method or code block.

For example, the following **BankAccount** setter method sets the value of the instance variable; `balance`.

```
balance: anAmount
"Sets the value of the balance attribute to
anAmount"

    balance := anAmount
```

25

To use the method, we send an instance of **BankAccount** a `balance:` message such as;
> `myAccount balance: 200`

The argument to `balance:` used here is `200` so, when the `balance:` method is executed, the method parameter, `anAmount`, acts like a temporary variable, referencing the object `200` throughout the execution of the method. Hence, within the method, the code effectively becomes;
> `balance := 200`

Of course, if we used a different argument for the message `balance:` sent to `myAccount`, this object would be referenced by `anAmount` when the method is run.

Because Smalltalk variables don't actually check whether the objects they reference are sensible in the context they are used, it would be quite possible to send the message;
> `myAccount balance: 'Frank Higgins'`

If the `balance:` method does not check whether the parameter is a valid number, it will assign `'Frank Higgins'` to `balance`, which will cause some difficultly when you try withdrawing cash!

The `balance:` method could and really should incorporate a check to make sure a valid number is being passed to it, perhaps by first sending the `anAmount` object an `isNumber` message, and then only changing the balance if all is okay.
The fact that the parameter passed to `balance:` must be a valid number is called a *precondition*.

Code blocks are a bit like mini-methods, and they too can have parameters. A block argument is similar to a temporary variable but is used within a block. It is prefixed with a `:` (colon) and is declared at the beginning of the block. It is separated from the statements in the block by a `|` (vertical bar).

In the expression series on the following page, the block iterates five times with the parameter, `num`, referencing each of the receiver array elements in turn; ie `2` on the first iteration, `4` on the second, `6` on the third, then `8`, and then `10`. `sum` finally references the sum of all these numbers;
> `(2 + 4 + 6 + 8 + 10) = 30.`

(Note that the block argument `num` does not need to be declared at the beginning of the expression series.)

```
"Sums the numbers 2, 4, 6, 8, 10"
|sum|
#(2 4 6 8 10) do: [:num | sum := sum + num].
^sum
```

Also see:
**+, -, *, /, **, //, **

Arithmetic operators

Arithmetic operations can be carried out using any of the following binary message selectors. The receiver and argument can each be any **Number** object.

+	"additon"
-	"subtraction"
*	"multiplication"
/	"division"
**	"to the power of"
//	"truncated division"
\\	"remainder from division"

Also see:
#, Collection, String

Array

Array is a Smalltalk class. It is a kind of **Collection**. See *Collection* for class hierarchy.

Objects of any kind can be placed in an instance of **Array**, including other arrays.
A mixture of different objects can be placed in a single array, and can be in any order. However, each element is indexed using an integer value to denote its position in the array. The index numbering begins at 1.
An instance of **Array** can hold any number of objects, but its size is defined when it is created and this cannot be changed later.
An **Array** object can contain duplicate elements.

The following array contains four different objects.

1	2	3	4
3.14	5	$A	'Eric'

Creation
You can create an instance of **Array** by sending a `new:` message to the **Array** class.

The following statement creates an empty instance of **Array** with space for three elements.

```
myArray := Array new: 3
```

This can be represented diagrammatically;

```
              1     2     3
myArray ---> nil | nil | nil
```

If an array is to contain only literals, it can be created by specifying the elements inside parentheses and prefixing with #.

```
myArray := #(5 2 5 7)
```

Adding elements
To add elements to an **Array** instance, send an `at: put:` message.

```
|myArray|
myArray := Array new:3.
myArray at: 1 put: 5.
myArray at: 2 put: 'Eric'.
myArray at: 3 put: 24
```

The above program creates an instance of **Array**, then adds three elements resulting in `myArray` referencing (5 'Eric' 24).

(Note that we cannot add any further objects to `myArray` because its size is fixed at three elements.)

Retrieval
To retrieve the object at a particular index in an array, send the **Array** instance an `at:` message. The following statement answers the object at array index 2.

```
myArray at: 2
```

Size
To determine the number of elements in an **Array** object, send it the `size` message.

```
myArray size
```

Iteration
To iterate over the elements in an instance of **Array**, you can use a `do:` message.
The following creates an instance of **Array** containing five integer numbers, and then iterates through the contents to calculate their total.

```
|myArray total|
total := 0.
myArray := #(5 2 5 7 3).
myArray do:
        [:element | total := total + element].
^total printString
```

Use
An **Array** instance is useful for managing an indexed list where the index is to be an integer value. The size of the list must be known in advance as arrays cannot grow or shrink, although they can contain elements that are `nil` (ie reference no valid object).

Array objects can contain elements that are themselves arrays. This is essential for creating multi-dimensional arrays. A table with, say, 20 rows and 10 columns can be created using an array of 20 elements, each of which is an array of 10 elements.

Assignment

Also see:
:=, Expressions

Variables are labels used to reference objects. We can change the object to which a variable refers by assignment. After assignment, we say that the object is assigned to the variable. The assignment operator is :=.

In the following example, the string object `'Eric'` is assigned to the variable `name`, so that `name` now references this object.
Assignment statement;

        name := 'Eric'

Diagrammatic view;

        name --→ 'Eric'

Message arguments are assigned (or, more correctly, bound) to the corresponding method parameters when a binary or keyword message-send is executed.

Association

Also see:
->, Dictionary

Association is a Smalltalk class.

Class hierarchy:

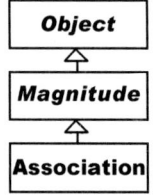

Association is used to define the elements of a **Dictionary** object. Objects of class **Association** can be placed in an instance of **Dictionary**.

An instance of **Dictionary** can hold any number of **Association** objects, and will grow or shrink appropriately as elements are added or removed.

Each **Association** instance consists of a *key-value* pair. *Values* can be of any class. In principle the *keys* can also be of any class but, in practice, they are most commonly **Integer**, **String** or **Symbol**.

Creation
You can create an instance of **Association** by sending a `new` message to the **Association** class.

The following statement creates an empty instance of **Association** with `key` and `value` both set to `nil`.

```
myAssociation := Association new
```

The `key: value:` message can be used to create and initialize an **Association** object. Also see entry for `->`.

The following creates an instance of **Association** (`#emp1->'Peters'`) and assigns it to the variable `myAssociation`.

```
myAssociation := Association key: #emp1
                             value: 'Peters'
```

Retrieval
To retrieve the value from an **Association** object, you can use the `value` message.

```
myAssociation value
```

To retrieve the key, use the `key` message.

```
myAssociation key
```

31

Attribute

Also see:
Behaviour, Objects

An attribute is a single piece of data or information that an object or class holds. Attributes are represented by class, instance and class instance variables.

For example, if the useful distinguishing attributes of a person are deemed to be name, age, and gender, then corresponding instance variables; `name`, `age`, and `gender` in class **Person** can be used to represent them.

Bag

Also see:
Collection, Set

Bag is a Smalltalk class. It is a subclass of **Collection**.
See *Collection* for class hierarchy.

Objects of any kind can be placed in an instance of **Bag** and it can hold any number of objects. It grows and shrinks in size as required.
Bag is very similar to **Set** but, unlike **Set**, it can contain duplicates. Its elements are unordered and not indexed.

Creation
You can create an instance of **Bag** by sending a `new` message to the class **Bag**.
The following statement creates an empty instance of **Bag**.

```
myBag := Bag new
```

Adding elements
To add elements to a **Bag** instance, send an `add:` message for each item to be added.

```
|myBag|
myBag := Bag new.
myBag add: 3.
myBag add: 'Eric'
```

The above program creates an instance of **Bag** and adds two elements, resulting in `myBag` referencing the **Bag** (3 `'Eric'`).

Size
To determine the number of elements in a **Bag** object, send it the `size` message as follows.

```
myBag size
```

Iteration
To iterate over the elements in an instance of **Bag**, you can use a `do:` message. The following program creates an instance of **Bag**, puts four integer numbers inside, and then iterates through the contents to calculate their total.

```
|myBag total|
total := 0.
myBag := Bag new.
myBag add: 4; add: 6; add: 3; add: 4.
myBag do: [:element | total := total + element].
^total printString
```

Use
A **Bag** instance is useful for managing a list that requires no particular ordering, can grow and shrink in size, and can contain duplicate elements.

Also see:
   Attributes, Objects

Behaviour

The behaviour of an object describes what it does when messages are sent to it. The instance and class methods defined in a class determine the behaviour. When a message is sent to a class instance, the code in the instance method corresponding to the message is carried out.
When a class itself receives a message, it is the corresponding class method that is executed. The code in these methods determines what actions are taken and hence collectively define behaviour.

There is also a class called **Behavior**. It is an abstract class that defines and implements the common protocol for all other classes. For example, the instance creation method `new` is inherited from **Behavior**. See *Metaclass* for more information.

Binary message

Also see:
Keyword message, Messages, Unary message

Binary message expressions consist of a message selector that can be either one or two characters long, followed by an argument.

For example in the binary message expression;
```
3 + 6
```

the number `3` is the receiver, and it is being sent the binary message `+ 6`.

This is similar in action to the keyword message expression;
```
3 add: 6
```

However, `3 + 6` conforms to the conventional way of writing arithmetic expressions, so is easier to read.

Binary message selectors can contain any of the characters:
```
+  -  *  /  \  <  >  =  @  %  |  &  ?  !  ,
```

The characters; `+ - * / ** // \\` are arithmetic binary selectors, and; `== = ~~ ~= < > <= >= & |` provide logical comparisons.

The characters; `@   ->` are used for object creation.

The binary message expression;
```
4 >= 2
```

compares the receiver `4` with the argument `2` to see if `4` is greater than, or equal to, `2`. In this case, the answer is, of course, `true`.

The next expression may look strange but it is also a binary message expression.
```
'Small'  ,  'talk'
```

The receiver is the string `'Small'`. The message selector is `,` which means concatenate (ie join two strings of characters together to form one). The argument is `'talk'`, which is another string. The answer produced is the two strings concatenated, ie; `'Smalltalk'`.

Also see:
**[ ], Boolean condition block,
Conditional expressions, Iteration**

Block

Smalltalk allows a block of code to be treated as an object. A block is an instance of the class **BlockClosure**.

Putting code into a block is a way of deferring its execution to be under the control of the Smalltalk environment at run time.
A block of code is enclosed in [ ] (square brackets) and executes when it is sent the message `value`, `value:` or `value: value:`, depending on the number of block arguments.

In the following code, to sum two integers, the receiver is an instance of **BlockClosure** and it is sent the message `value`. Temporary variables are declared at the start of the block. The answer returned in this case will be 8.

```
[|a b sum|
a := 3.
b := 5.
sum := a + b.
^sum] value
```

In the next example, one of the variables is treated as a block parameter. The argument of the `value:` message (ie 3) is bound to the block parameter `a` when the expression is evaluated. This allows us to pass an object into a block from the outside.

```
[:a |
|b sum|
b := 5.
sum := a + b.
^sum] value: 3
```

In the third example, both variables, `a` and `b`, are treated as block parameters. The `value: value:` message selector takes two arguments, which are bound to their respective block parameters.

```
[:a :b |
|sum|
sum := a + b.
^sum] value: 3 value: 5
```

35

Blocks are often used to specify the code to be executed by Smalltalk if some boolean condition is met.
In the following conditional expression, blocks are required as arguments to ifTrue: ifFalse: so that the Smalltalk system can evaluate the appropriate block at run time.

```
(age < 18)
    ifTrue: [^'Too young to vote']
    ifFalse: [^'Too old for short trousers']
```

Blocks are also used in boolean expressions such as;

```
(age > 17 and: [age < 20])
```

In this case the block is only executed if the receiver age > 17 evaluates to true.

Blocks are also commonly used for iteration. See *Iteration*.

Boolean

Also see:
Boolean condition block, Conditional expressions, Logical operators

Boolean is an abstract class. It is used to implement the behaviour common to its subclasses; **True** and **False**.

Class hierarchy:

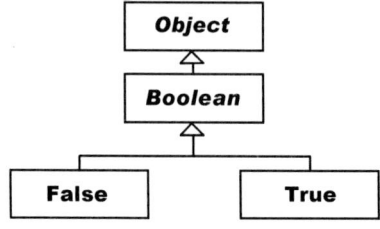

True has a single instance; true.
False has a single instance; false.

The object instances `true` and `false` respond to message selectors such as;
    ifTrue:
    ifFalse:
    ifTrue: ifFalse:
    ifFalse: ifTrue:

Also see:
Block, Conditional expressions

Boolean condition block

A boolean condition block is any expression within `[ ]` (square brackets) that evaluates to `true` or `false`.
A condition block is used as the receiver of `whileTrue:` and `whileFalse:` messages.

The format for use is;
    [*Boolean condition block*]
        whileTrue: [*Block to execute repeatedly
                    while condition is true*]

For example, in the following code, the boolean condition block is `[count < 3]`. The final value of `sum` returned is `6`.

    |count sum|
    count := 0.
    sum := 0.
    [count < 3]
        whileTrue: [count := count + 1.
                    sum := sum + count].
    ^sum

The condition block is re-evaluated on each iteration until it answers `false`.

Number of Iterations	count	condition block value
1	0	true
2	1	true
3	2	true
4	3	false

The code block;
```
[count := count + 1.
    sum := sum + count]
```
is executed three times, summing 1 + 2 + 3 before the condition block evaluates to `false` and iteration stops.

BOSS

The BOSS acronym denotes the *Binary Object Streaming Service*, which stores objects in coded format in a binary file.
BOSS is used to store one or more objects to disk. It is possible to store an entire collection as a single object.
The binary files that are produced by BOSS are compact in size and quick to store and to access.

Bytecode

Also see:
Compiled language, Interpreted language

Programs written in high-level languages must be converted into the machine code suitable for the specific type of processor to be used. This means that programs written in compiled languages need to be separately compiled for each processor type on which they are to be run. This is clearly bad news for program portability.

The problem can be overcome by using an appropriate Interpreter on each machine to be used for the program. However, Interpreters slow down program execution.

A compromise solution used for Java, and by some Smalltalk environments, is to first compile the high-level source code to produce an intermediate code called bytecode.

Each machine on which the bytecode is to be executed must still run an Interpreter that converts the bytecode into appropriate machine code but bytecode is designed to be efficiently interpreted as it is executed. A processor running such an interpreter is called a *Virtual Machine*.

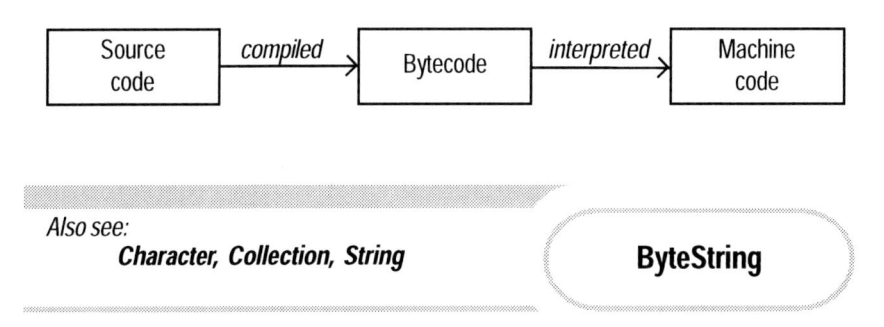

```
┌──────────┐  compiled   ┌──────────┐  interpreted  ┌──────────┐
│  Source  │ ──────────> │ Bytecode │ ────────────> │  Machine │
│   code   │             │          │               │   code   │
└──────────┘             └──────────┘               └──────────┘
```

Also see:
Character, Collection, String

ByteString

Instances of class **ByteString** are indexed collections of characters. See *Collection* for class hierarchy.

These characters are instances of class **Character** and are stored as bytes. (Note that a byte is a group of 8 binary digits, or bits.)

String is an abstract class, and **String** objects are actually instances of the concrete class **ByteString**. **ByteString** is an indirect subclass of **String**.

To illustrate, inspecting the string `'Hello'` shows its class to be **ByteString**.

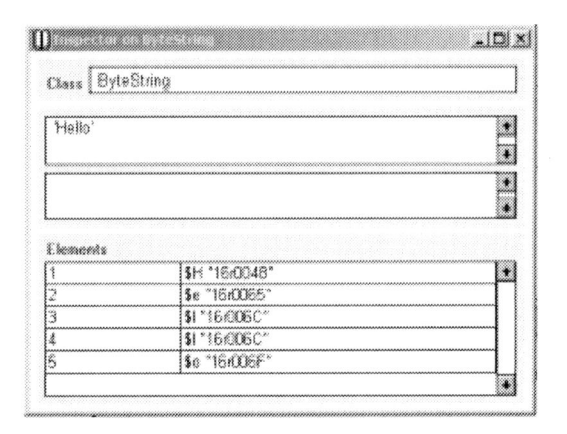

39

Character

Also see:
$, String

Instances of class **Character** are characters from the ASCII set. The class **Character** defines the protocol for these.

Class hierarchy:

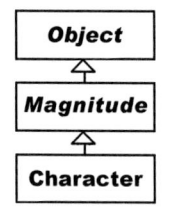

```
    Object
      △
   Magnitude
      △
   Character
```

Instances of **Character** do not have to be created explicitly as they are pre-existing, immutable objects.

References to characters can be made by prefixing the character with $.

Thus;
```
$A      "represents A"
$$      "represents $"
$       "represents Space character"
```

Sending a conversion message to an integer (representing the desired character's ASCII value) can also be used to produce references to characters.

For example;
```
9 asCharacter          "answers the tab character"
```

There are a number of methods available for use with instances of **Character**, including;

```
$e asUppercase      "answers $E"
$E asLowercase      "answers $e"
$i isVowel          "answers true"
$h isUppercase      "answers false"
$h isLowercase      "answers true"
$3 isDigit          "answers true"
```

Also see:
Class browser, Class hierarchy, Class library, Metaclass, Subclass, Superclass

Class

A class is a template from which objects are created. The class defines their common attributes, behaviour and relationships.

Consider the class of objects we call Cars. Cars are characterised by attributes such as make and colour, amongst others. My car is a specific instance of a Car. Its attribute values happen to be Volvo and Blue. Its behaviour, in common with other cars, includes acceleration and braking.

Classes group objects according to some common types of attribute and behaviour.

In object-oriented software, a class definition describes the instance and class variables of its member objects, and all the methods that implement their behaviour. Thus, a software representation of our simplified Car class would define the class **Car**, along with instance variables to describe its attributes; `make` and `colour`, and include the instance methods `accelerate: anAmount` and `brake: anAmount` to implement its behaviour. We can then use this template to create as many individual instances of **Car** as we require.

New classes can be defined using the tools in the Smalltalk *Class browser*, or can be done in the *Workspace* by sending an appropriate message to the superclass.

For our example;

```
Object subclass: #Car
    instanceVariableNames: 'make colour'
    classVariableNames: ''
    poolDictionaries: ''
```

There is a class called **Class** that is the superclass of all Smalltalk classes. It defines the common protocol for defining and accessing class variables and pool dictionaries. See *Metaclass* and *Global variables* for further information.

41

Class browser

Also see:
Class, Debugger, Inspector, Workspace

The *Class browser* is a utility provided by the Smalltalk development environment enabling you to view all the available classes with their variable and method definitions.

The following illustration shows the LearningWorks™ *Class browser*.

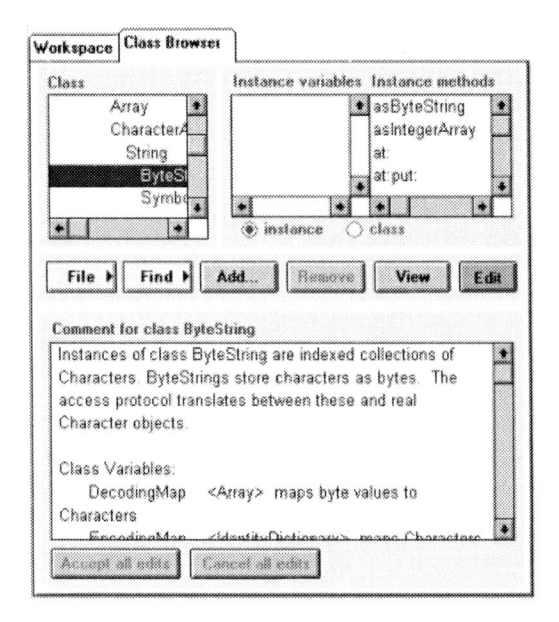

Class hierarchy

Also see:
Class, Class browser, Class library, Subclass, Superclass

Every class, apart from the **Object** class, is derived from some other class. The relationships between subclasses and superclasses form a hierarchical tree structure with **Object** at its root (or base class).

The following diagram shows a small portion of the Smalltalk class hierarchy.

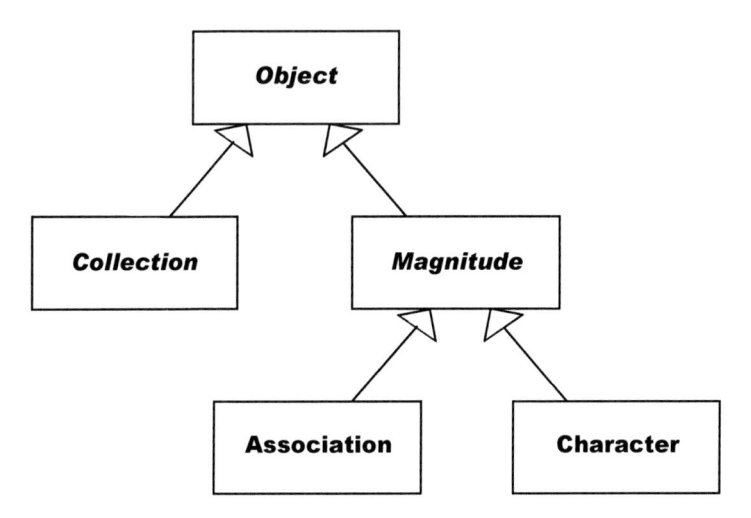

```
                    ┌──────────┐
                    │  Object  │
                    └──────────┘
                     △        △
                    ╱          ╲
          ┌────────────┐   ┌────────────┐
          │ Collection │   │ Magnitude  │
          └────────────┘   └────────────┘
                            △        △
                           ╱          ╲
                ┌─────────────┐   ┌───────────┐
                │ Association │   │ Character │
                └─────────────┘   └───────────┘
```

(Note that, unlike trees in nature, the root is at the top; similar to a family tree.)

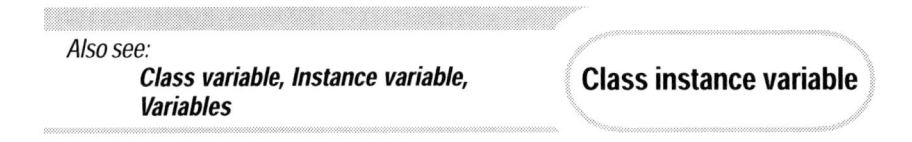

Also see:
Class variable, Instance variable, Variables

Class instance variable

Class variables are variables associated with a class rather than its instances. For any given class variable, only one copy is held for the whole class. Its value is accessible from all the methods of the class, its instances, the subclasses and their instances.

All instances of a class, and the class itself, share the same class variables. The class variables and their values are inherited by all the subclasses. Thus, if a subclass modifies the value of a class variable held by its superclass, all other classes derived from the superclass see the change.

Sometimes subclasses need to override a class variable. In other words, they need their own copy that is not affected by changes made from other subclasses. Unfortunately, with class variables this is not possible. All we can do is ignore the inherited class variable and create a replacement in the subclass.

However, class instance variables overcome this problem. These are, in a sense, instance variables belonging to a class.

Class instance variables are inherited by the subclasses but, unlike class variables, each subclass can assign its own value.

Class instance variables can only be referenced by class methods, NOT by instance methods.

Assume we have a **Machine** class, instances of which represent a computer-controlled machine in an engineering works. The class defines class variable Count, which maintains a count of the total number of machines in the works. Every time a new machine is introduced or removed, the value of Count is updated.
Now let's assume that two subclasses; **Lathe** and **Mill** are to be derived from the class **Machine**.

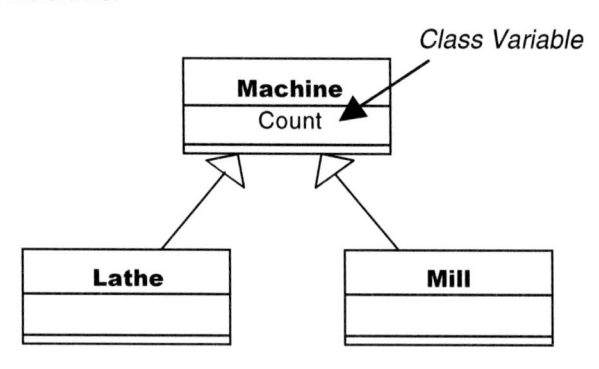

```
                    Class Variable
        Machine
         Count
       ╱       ╲
   Lathe         Mill
```

Instances of **Lathe** and instances of **Mill** can all access the class variable Count inherited from **Machine**. So, if a new instance of **Lathe** is created, Count is incremented, and likewise for a new instance of **Mill**.

However, what if we want to record the total number of **Lathe** instances separately from the total for **Mill**?
Both classes inherit Count but, if an instance of either updates its value, both will see the change.
To overcome this problem, we could create new class variables in the subclasses.

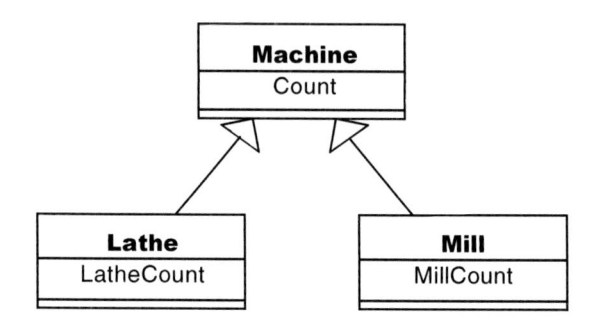

```
        Machine
         Count
       ╱       ╲
   Lathe         Mill
 LatheCount    MillCount
```

Instances of **Lathe** would update `LatheCount`, which would keep count of the **Lathe** instances. Similarly, `MillCount` would keep the total of **Mill** instances. This is okay, but has the disadvantage that subclasses still inherit the `Count` class variable that they don't need. Also, any future subclasses of **Lathe** and **Mill** will, perhaps unnecessarily, inherit their class variables. The problem is overcome if we make `count` a class instance variable. (Notice that I have changed its initial letter to lowercase, since it is no longer a class variable.)

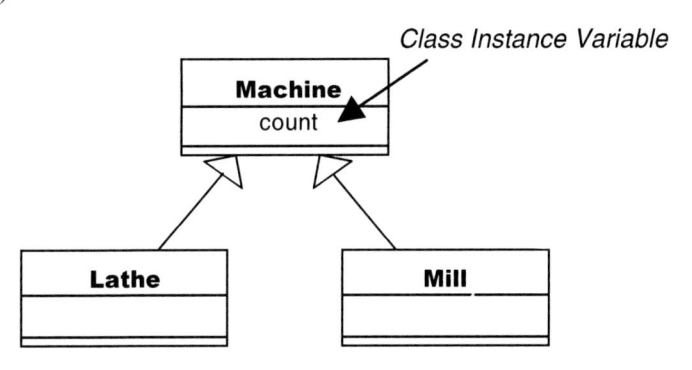

Class Instance Variable

```
         Machine
         count
        /      \
     Lathe     Mill
```

Now the subclasses inherit their own copy of the variable so, if **Lathe** updates the value of its `count`, it does not affect **Mill**'s copy of `count`.

Class instance variables can be created in the *Workspace* by sending an `instanceVariableNames:` message to modify the meta-class. In our example, we would use the expression;

    `(Machine class) instanceVariableNames: 'count'`

Also see:
    Class, Class browser

Class library

A class library is a collection of related classes. These classes are made available for reuse.

For example, a class library may exist containing classes suitable for 3D graphic objects such as cubes and spheres. These can then be incorporated in new applications without having to rewrite the complex code required to manipulate 3D objects.

Class method

Also see:
Instance method, Messages, Methods

Class methods define the code executed when a message is sent to a class.

The receiver of a message corresponding to a class method must always be a class, rather than an instance of the class.

In the following statement, the class **Set** is being sent the `new` message, which causes the code defined in class method `new` to be executed.

    mySet := Set new

In this case, the class creates a new instance of **Set**, which is then assigned to the variable `mySet`.

Class methods are mainly used for instance creation but have other uses. For example, the class **Date** defines the class method;
    leapYear: yearInteger

which answers 1 if `yearInteger` is a leap year, and 0 otherwise. For example;
    Date leapYear: 2000   "answers 1"
    Date leapYear: 2003   "answers 0"

Class variable

Also see:
Class instance variable, Constant, Instance variable, Variables

Class variables are variables held by a class, rather than instances of the class. All instances of a class, and the class itself, share the same class variables. Class variables and their values are both inherited by subclasses, and they can be referenced from instance and class methods by referring to the name of the class variable.
By convention, class variable names begin with an uppercase letter.

For example, suppose we have a **Machine** class with instance variable `usage`. Each instance of **Machine** represents a computer-controlled machine in an

46

engineering works. Every time we create an instance of **Machine**, it will have its own private instance variable, usage, the value of which keeps track of the number of items produced by the machine over its lifetime.

Now let's say we want to keep track of the total daily production of items from all the instances of **Machine** that have been created. We could do this by introducing a class variable called DailyCount, which maintains a single daily total for the factory, and is reset to zero each day.

Because DailyCount is a class variable, there is just one variable for the whole **Machine** class, rather than a separate copy for every instance of the class. To keep the correct totals, every time an instance of **Machine** updates its usage variable, the value of DailyCount is also updated. All machines have their own usage variable but all share the same DailyCount variable.

In the following diagram, machine1 and machine2 are instances of **Machine**. They each have their own usage variable, but both have access to the shared variable; DailyCount.

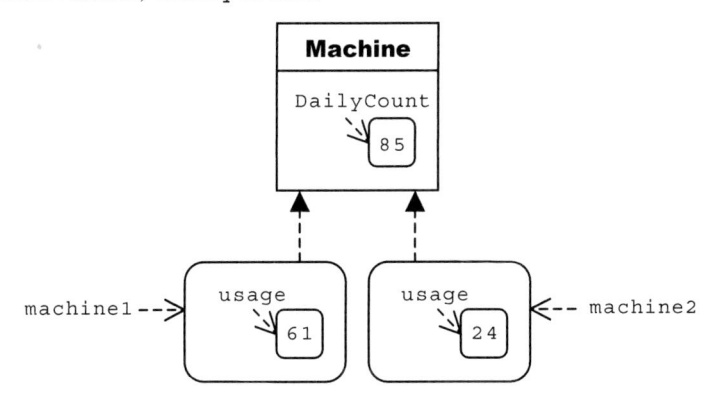

```
                    ┌──────────────┐
                    │   Machine    │
                    ├──────────────┤
                    │  DailyCount  │
                    │       ↘      │
                    │        ┌──┐  │
                    │        │85│  │
                    │        └──┘  │
                    └──────────────┘
                       ▲        ▲
                       ┆        ┆
                   ┌───────┐ ┌───────┐
                   │ usage │ │ usage │
        machine1-->│   ↘   │ │   ↘   │<-- machine2
                   │  ┌──┐ │ │  ┌──┐ │
                   │  │61│ │ │  │24│ │
                   │  └──┘ │ │  └──┘ │
                   └───────┘ └───────┘
```

Class variables can be defined as part of the class definition as follows:
```
Object subclass: #Machine
    instanceVariableNames: 'usage'
    classVariableNames: 'DailyCount'
    poolDictionaries: ''
```

A class variable can also be used to hold a constant that needs to be available to all instances of the class. For example, the mathematical constant π (Pi).

Subclass methods can modify inherited class variables but generally should not because it would change the value seen by all other subclasses.
If a subclass needs a different value, we could give it its own class variable. Methods that access the class then need to be overridden.

47

Collection

Also see:
Array, Bag, Dictionary, OrderedCollection,
Set, SortedCollection, String, Symbol

Handling lists is a common requirement of computer software. For example, a small business system might need to maintain lists of its customers and products. Smalltalk provides a set of **Collection** classes for this purpose.
A **Collection** object maintains a collection of elements, each of which is a pointer to an object.

Class hierarchy:

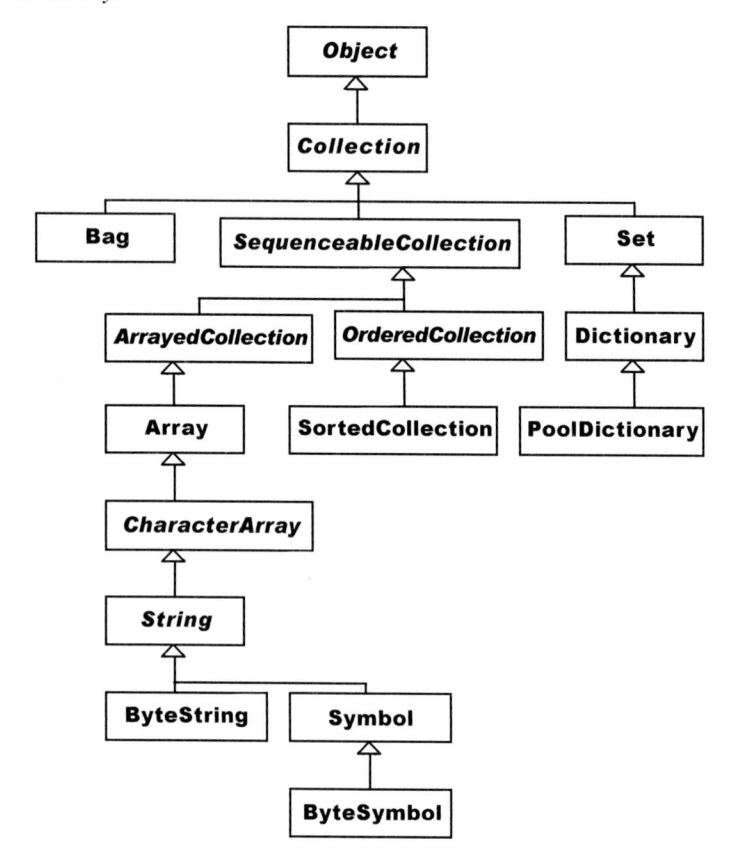

```
                         Object
                           ▲
                           |
                       Collection
                           ▲
           ┌───────────────┼───────────────┐
          Bag    SequenceableCollection   Set
                           ▲               ▲
                ┌──────────┼──────────┐    |
         ArrayedCollection  OrderedCollection  Dictionary
                ▲                ▲             ▲
               Array      SortedCollection  PoolDictionary
                ▲
          CharacterArray
                ▲
              String
                ▲
         ┌──────┴──────┐
      ByteString     Symbol
                        ▲
                    ByteSymbol
```

Some collection classes can be indexed so that you can refer to the element at a specific location in the collection, whereas others are unindexed.
Some collections are variable in size so they can grow and shrink as items are added or removed, whereas others are of fixed size.

Some collections can be ordered, whereas others are unordered.
Some collections can contain duplicate elements, whereas others cannot.
Some collections can contain elements that are of any class, whereas others can only contain one specific class of object.

The above factors need to be taken into account when selecting the most appropriate kind of collection to use for any given purpose.
The following table summarises the **Collection** classes and their properties.

Collection Class	Order	Integer indexing	Size	Duplicates	Class of content
Array	Unsorted	Yes	Fixed	Allowed	Any
Bag	Unsorted	No	Variable	Allowed	Any but nil
Dictionary	Unsorted	No	Variable	Not allowed	Association
OrderedCollection	Unsorted	Yes	Variable	Allowed	Any
Set	Unsorted	No	Variable	Not allowed	Any but nil
SortedCollection	Sorted	Yes	Variable	Allowed	Any
String	Unsorted	Yes	Fixed	Allowed	Character

Also see:
   Methods

Comment

Any text enclosed in double quotes within a Smalltalk program is treated as a comment. Comments are for the benefit of the reader and are ignored by the compiler.

Comments are very important for clarifying the meaning of program code. They can explain the pre and post-conditions, and the purpose of a piece of code, along with other useful information.

In the following method, a comment is used to explain its function and authorship.

```
age: aNumber
"Setter method for age.
 Sets the age instance variable to the value
 aNumber.  Answers the receiver.
 —Version 1
 —Written by Fred Higgins 23 May 2003"
     age := aNumber
```

Compiled language

Also see:
Bytecode, Interpreted language

Machine code is the program code that can be executed directly on a computer's processor. Programs written in high-level languages must be converted to machine code from the original source code.
Compiled languages are high-level programming languages that must be converted to machine code as a distinct process before they are run. The conversion from source code is carried out using a program called a Compiler. The advantage of this, as opposed to a language that is interpreted, is that syntax errors in the source code can be identified and corrected before running the program. Also, once your program is compiled, it should execute efficiently, and can be repeatedly run without recompiling.

Concatenate

Also see:
, , Array, OrderedCollection, SortedCollection, String, Symbol

We can concatenate strings by combining them into a single string. The binary message selector , (comma) can be used for this, as in;

    'Small' , 'talk'   "answers 'Smalltalk' "

or using the keyword message selector concatenate: as in;

    'Small' concatenate: 'talk'

In fact, the binary message selector , can be applied to an object of any class that inherits from **SequenceableCollection** including; **Array**, **Symbol**, **String**, **OrderedCollection** or **SortedCollection**.

The following program returns the **OrderedCollection** (1 2 3 4).

```
|myCollection yourCollection|
myCollection := OrderedCollection new.
yourCollection := OrderedCollection new.
myCollection add: 1; add: 2.
yourCollection add: 3; add: 4.
^ myCollection , yourCollection
```

Also see:
**Block, Boolean,
Boolean condition block, Iteration**

Conditional expressions

Conditional expressions allow branching during the execution of program code. The following keyword selectors can be used;

```
ifTrue:, ifFalse:, ifTrue: ifFalse:, ifFalse: ifTrue:
```

The receiver must be an expression that evaluates to `true` or `false`.

```
(age >= 18)
    ifTrue: [^'A glass of lager please']
    ifFalse: [^'A glass of orange juice please']
```

In the above conditional expression, the boolean expression `(age >= 18)` is evaluated first. This becomes the receiver of the `ifTrue: ifFalse:` message, which evaluates the `ifTrue:` block of code inside the square brackets if the boolean expression is `true`, and evaluates the `ifFalse:` code block if the expression is `false`.

Sometimes only an `ifTrue:` block is required. In the following example, if the boolean expression is `false`, nothing is done.

```
(age >= 18)
    ifTrue: [^'A glass of lager please']
```

And sometimes only an `ifFalse:` block is wanted. In the next example, if the boolean expression is `true`, nothing is done.

```
(age >= 18)
    ifFalse: [^'A glass of orange juice please']
```

It is possible to nest expressions within one another. For example;

```
(age >=18)
    ifTrue:  [ ^'A glass of lager please']
    ifFalse: [(age >= 2)
                ifTrue: [^'A glass of orange
                                   juice please']
                ifFalse: [^'A bottle of warm
                                   milk please']]
```

If `age` is `18` or over, then lager is requested.
If `age` is between `2` and `17`, then orange juice is required.
If `age` is less than `2`, then warm milk is wanted.

Constant

Also see:
Class variable

Constants are objects that never change value. For example, the value of π (Pi) in mathematics is a constant.
If a class needs to define a constant, this is usually done in the class itself. In Smalltalk, a class variable can be used, but there is no mechanism to ensure a constant is fully protected from change.

Conversion

Also see:
Dialog, Float, Integer, Number, String

When Smalltalk is presented with an arithmetic expression that contains a mixture of classes, it attempts to evaluate the expression in a way that does not lose information.

For example, the following message expression multiplies an integer by a floating-point number.

```
4 * 2.4
```

Evaluating the above, Smalltalk creates an instance of **Float** from the integer 4, and answers the **Float** instance; 9.6.

It is also possible to convert a number from one class to another explicitly.

asInteger
To convert to **Integer** use the message asInteger.
```
2.7 asInteger        "truncates 2.7 and answers 2"
-2.7 asInteger       "truncates -2.7 and answers -2"
```

(Note that some implementations of asInteger may round the result rather than truncate.)

asFloat
To convert to **Float** use the message asFloat.
```
2 asFloat        "answers 2.0"
```

asNumber
To convert a **String** to a **Number** object, use the message `asNumber`.

    `'2.7' asNumber`   "answers the **Float** instance `2.7`"
    `'4' asNumber`   "answers the **SmallInteger** instance `4`"

This is useful when obtaining number input from a text entry box at the user interface. Numbers are entered at the interface as strings and need to be converted before they can be used in arithmetic calculations.

asRational
To convert an instance of **Float** into an instance of **Fraction** use the `asRational` message.

    `0.5 asRational`   "answers the **Fraction** instance `(1/2)`"

Other conversion methods that should be available in your Smalltalk environment include;
    `asString` for converting **Number** to **String**.

And for converting between collection classes;
    `asArray`
    `asBag`
    `asSet`
    `asOrderedCollection`
    `asSortedCollection`

Also see:
    Time

Date

Date is a class provided by Smalltalk systems.

Class hierarchy:

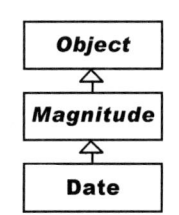

    Object
      △
    Magnitude
      △
    Date

An instance of class **Date** represents a specific day since the start of the Julian calendar.
To answer today's date, send the message `today` to class **Date**.
   `Date today`

To create an instance of **Date** representing a specific date, and to assign it to a variable;
   `birthday := Date newDay: 14 monthNumber: 9`
   `                                       year: 1952`

There is a variety of messages that can be sent to instances of **Date**.

`birthday day`	"answers the day of the year represented by the receiver; in this case `258`"
`birthday year`	"answers the year; in this case `1952`"
`birthday asDays`	"answers the number of days between January 1, 1901 and the receiver's day; in this case `18884`"
`birthday dateOfMonth`	"answers the day of the month that is represented by the receiver; in this case `14`"
`birthday monthName`	"answers the name of the month in which the receiver falls; in this case `#September`. Note the `#` prefix because this is an instance of class **Symbol**"
`birthday addDays: 21`	"answers a new **Date** that is `21` more days on from the receiver; in this case `October 5, 1952`"
`birthday weekday`	"answers the name of the day of the week on which the receiver falls; in this case `#Sunday`"

Date instances can also be compared;
   `anitaBirth := Date newDay: 21 monthNumber: 3`
   `                                       year: 1979.`
   `johnBirth  := Date newDay: 22 monthNumber: 3`
   `                                       year: 1979.`
   `anitaBirth = johnBirth      "answers false"`
   `anitaBirth < johnBirth      "answers true"`
   `anitaBirth > johnBirth      "answers false"`

Also see:
Errors, Inspector, Class browser, Workspace

Debugger

A *Debugger* allows you to trace processing during execution of a program. With it you can step through method code line by line, as it runs. You can also inspect variables and change their values if necessary. This makes life much easier when it comes to tracking down the causes of error.

Sending an object a `halt` message places a *Notifier* window on the screen, giving you the option to debug the program. The default *Notifier* message can be replaced by using a `halt: aString` message.

Selecting the **Debug** button in the *Notifier* window opens a *Debugger* window.

To illustrate a program trace using a debugger, I have set up the class **Person** with instance variables `name` and `age`, and will trace part of the initialisation of a new instance of **Person** referenced by the variable `aPerson`. I am using a LearningWorks™ *Debugger* for this but, whichever system you use, the principles will be similar.

Here's the class definition;

Class: **Person**
Instance variables: `name, age`

Setter instance methods:
```
name: aString
"Sets the name variable to reference aString.
Answers the receiver."
    name := aString

age: aNumber
"Sets the age variable to reference aNumber.
Answers the receiver."
    age := aNumber
```

Getter instance methods:
```
name
"Answers the name."
    ^ name
```

55

```
age
    "Answers the age."
    ^ age
```

Initialize instance method:
```
initialize
    "Initializes an instance of Person.  Answers the
    receiver."
    self halt: 'Stopping in Initialize'.
    self name: 'Anita'.
    self age: 21
```

Class method new:
```
new
    "Creates a new instance of Person.  Answers the
    new instance."
    ^super new initialize
```

Notice that, at the beginning of `initialize`, we are sending a `halt:` message to the newly created **Person** object.

Executing the code;

```
|aPerson|
aPerson := Person new
```

in the *Workspace* now opens a *Notifier* window.

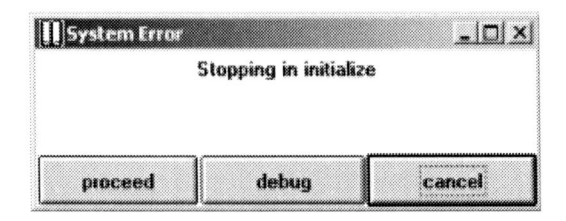

56

Pressing the **Debug** button opens a *Debugger*. The top panel shows the 'execution stack' which lists all the message-sends still being processed. The format is;

class of the receiver
　　>>the message

Notice, that the `halt:` message is selected because this is where execution halted.

Left-clicking on `Person>>initialize` and selecting the **Messages** tab takes us into the `initialize` method code, with highlighting on the currently executing message; ie `halt: 'Stopping in initialize'`.

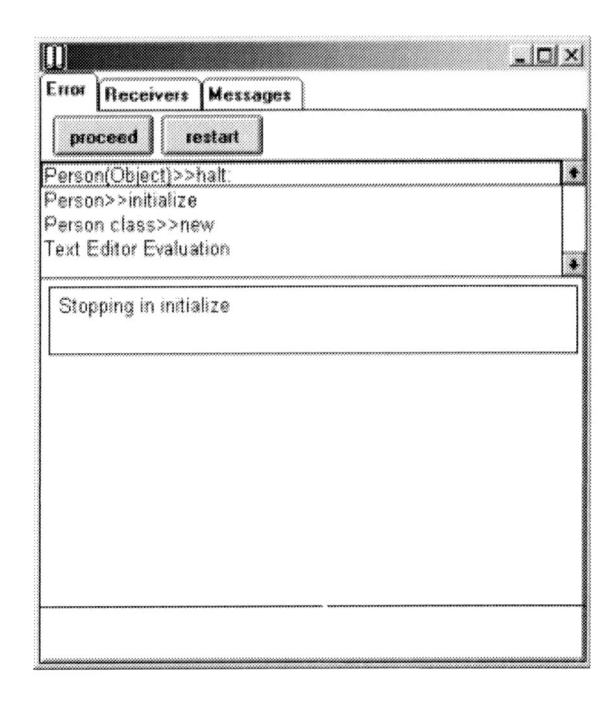

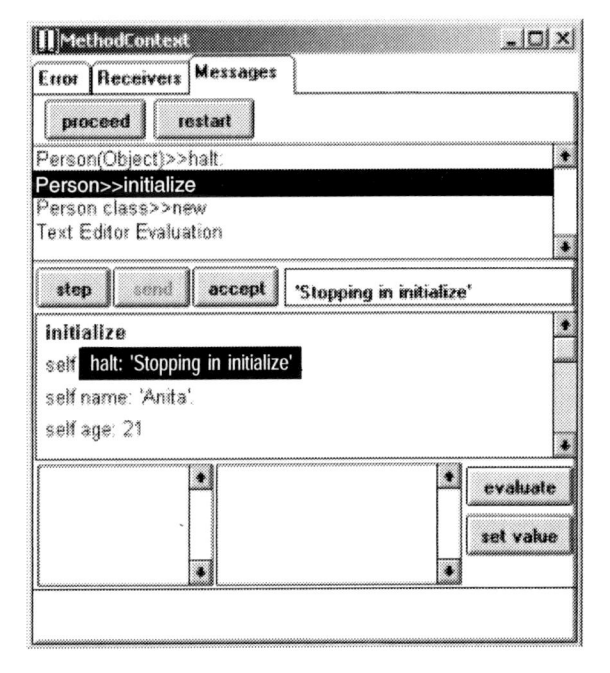

Pressing the **Step** button executes the next message-send, and the highlighting moves to the `name:` setter message;
   `name: 'Anita'.`

Pressing **Step** again, executes this message-send and the highlighting moves to the next message to be sent;
   `age: 21`

Notice that by pressing **Step**, we caused the `name:` setter method code to be executed without stepping line by line through its code.
This time we will move into the `age:` setter method by pressing the **Send** button instead of **Step**.

The *Debugger* now shows the `age:` method with execution halted on the
`age := aNumber` assignment statement.

We can view the current values of any variables or arguments in the lower panels. In this case, clicking once on `aNumber` shows its value is `21`. Clicking twice opens an *Inspector* on this object.

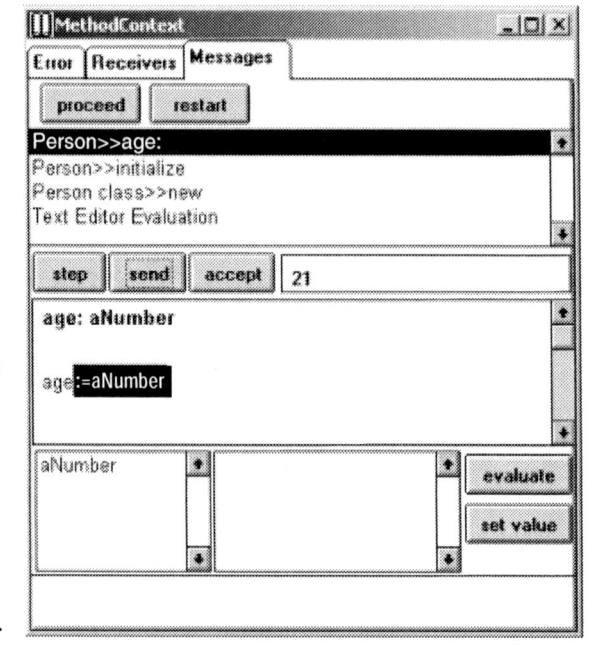

The **Receivers** page shows the state of the receiver; in this case; `aPerson`.

Clicking `name` shows its current value and, as it is a collection of character elements, also allows you to access each of its five ASCII coded elements by selecting their index numbers.

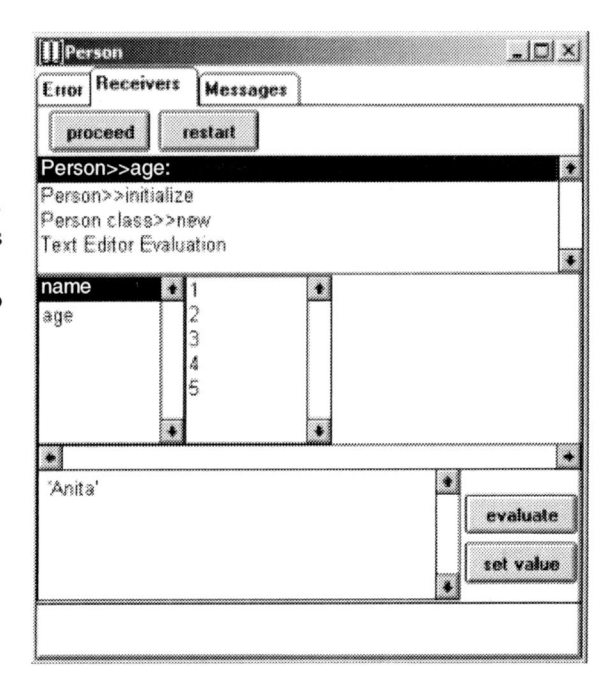

Selecting the `age` variable shows the current value is `nil`, because its value has not yet been initialised.

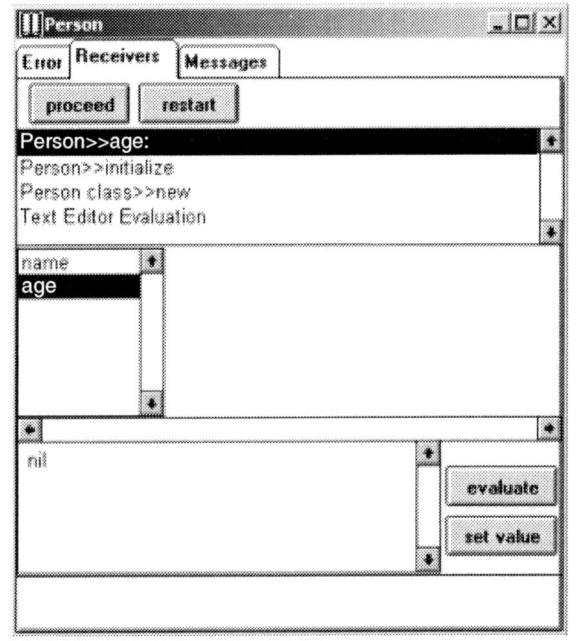

59

Back on the **Messages** page, pressing the **Step** button twice, completes execution of the `age:` setter method and the *Debugger* display returns to the `initialize` method with the small arrow head showing the message-send that has just finished. The small panel, centre right, shows a representation of the object returned by the last message-send. In this case; `'a Person'`.

Now checking `age` on the **Receivers** page shows its value has been set to `21`. The values referenced by variables can be altered at any stage by editing them in the *Debugger* and pressing the **set value** button.
The **proceed** button continues execution to the end.
The **restart** button resets all variables and restarts execution.

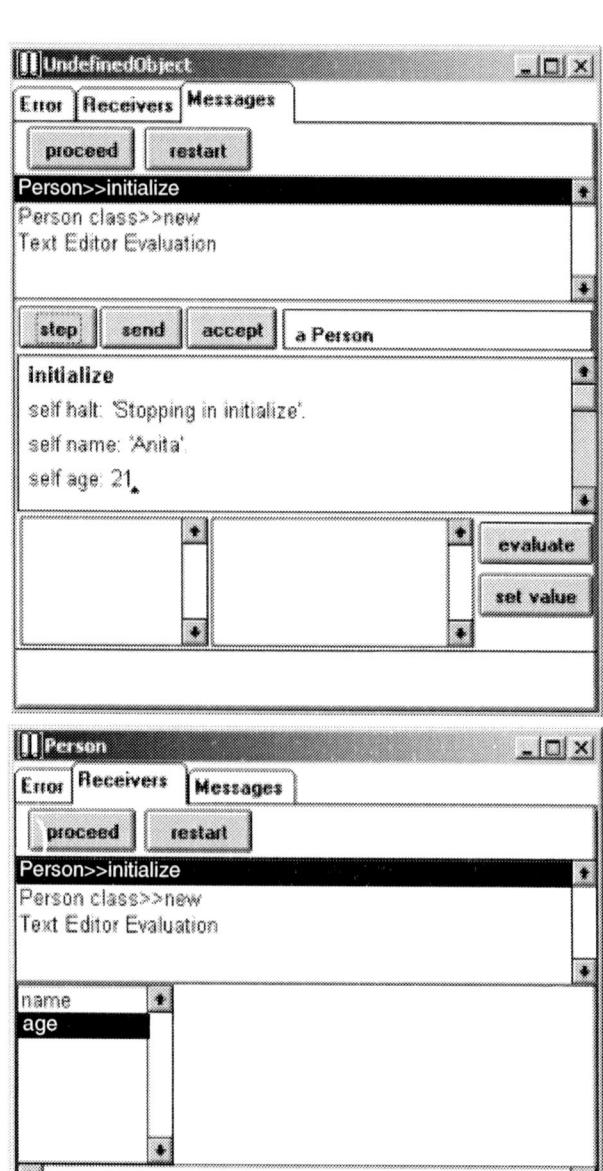

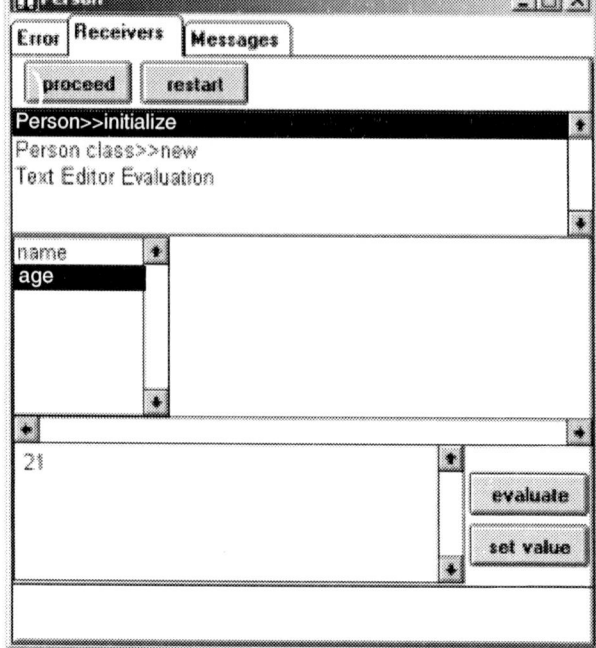

60

Also see:
Model View Controller, Models

Dependency mechanism

In a software application, the domain model comprises all the classes that are required to fulfil the underlying purpose of the application. It is commonly the case that the essential code of an application domain does not change much, whereas interfaces may be regularly updated, or alternative interfaces made available for different users. The classes that make up the interface are kept as independent as possible from those of the domain so we can alter either without disrupting the other.

For example, consider an application that monitors the temperature and oxygen level within an incubator. Let's assume that the incubator sensors take readings every few seconds. The temperature and oxygen levels are displayed on a monitor and their values are updated only when the sensors detect a change in the incubator environment. There is also an alarm, which sounds if the temperature goes outside set bounds.

In designing the software for this system, we might have an object to represent the incubator, another to handle display on the monitor, and a third for the alarm.

If the incubator object detects any change of state (ie change in temperature or oxygen level), it would need to notify the monitor object and the alarm object.

If later we added a new object representing a graph plotter to record changes in oxygen level, all the incubator object needs to do is add the graph plotter to its list of objects and notify it if any changes occur. We don't have to change the incubator class in any way.

We could have the monitor and alarm periodically checking the incubator readings but this is wasteful because, if they checked, say, every 30 seconds, it could be that several checks are made before any change occurs. Also, if a change does occur, it could be up to 30 seconds before it is discovered.

In this example, we say that the alarm, monitor and plotter objects are dependents or disciples of incubator, and the incubator is the parent or master.

We can make any object a dependent of another by sending the parent object an `addDependent:` message.

So;
>   anIncubator addDependent: aMonitor.
>   anIncubator addDependent: anAlarm.
>   anIncubator addDependent: aPlotter

would make the monitor (`aMonitor`), alarm (`anAlarm`) and plotter (`aPlotter`) dependents of the incubator (`anIncubator`).

When the state of parent (ie `anIncubator`) changes, it sends itself a `changed` message;
>   self changed

Here's the changed method, that is inherited by all classes, as it is implemented in the class **Object**;

> **changed**
> "Receiver changed in a general way; inform all the dependents by sending each dependent an update: message."
>   self changed: nil

Notice that this calls the `changed:` method which is;

> **changed: anAspectSymbol**
> "Receiver changed. The change is denoted by the argument anAspectSymbol. Usually the argument is a Symbol that is part of the dependent's change protocol, that is, some aspect of the object's behavior. Inform all of the dependents."
>   self changed: anAspectSymbol with: nil

And this in turn calls the `changed: with:` method;

> **changed: anAspectSymbol with: aParameter**
> "The receiver changed. The change is denoted by the argument anAspectSymbol. Usually the argument is a Symbol that is part of the dependent's change protocol, that is, some aspect of the object's behavior, and aParameter is additional information. Inform all of the dependents."
>   self myDependents update: anAspectSymbol
>   with: aParameter from: self

which now sends all the dependent objects an `update: with: from:` message.

All dependents need to implement their own `update: with: from:` method containing code for the actions each is to carry out when notified of a change to the parent.

A parent holds a dictionary of its dependents in the **Object** class variable called `DependentFields`. There is only one copy of this variable held by **Object**. Before a dependent is removed from the system, it should remove itself from this dictionary by sending its parent the message;

   `removeDependent: self.`

If this is not done, `DependentFields` becomes fuller and fuller with references to objects that no longer exist.

A better approach is to make any classes, that are to have dependents, subclasses of **Model** rather than **Object**.
The **Model** class provides automatic removal of dependency relationships when a parent is no longer in use and has been garbage collected by the system.

The class **Model** has a single instance variable called `dependents`. If you subclass any class that is to act as a parent, from **Model**, it will inherit the `dependents` instance variable. When the parent instance is no longer in use, its `dependents` collection will no longer exist.

The dependency mechanism provides a useful separation between a domain model and its user interfaces. When any change of state occurs to the objects comprising the underlying domain model, the interfaces are notified that a change has occurred, and what that change is. This means that it is straightforward to design a system in which a single domain model has several dependent interfaces.

Dialog

LearningWorks™ Smalltalk includes three types of dialog box. Class methods of the **Dialog** class are used to produce them.

Dialog warn
Sending the class **Dialog** a message using the keyword selector `warn:` produces a dialog warn box.

```
Dialog warn: 'This is a Dialog warn box'
```

and this is another, using a temporary variable to reference the string;

```
messageString:='This is another Dialog warn box'.
Dialog warn: messageString
```

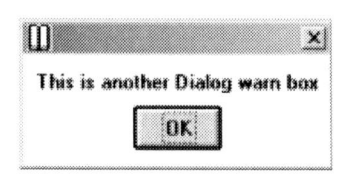

`Dialog warn:` answers `nil`, so the statement;

```
reply:= Dialog warn: 'This is a Dialog warn box'
```

assigns `nil` to the variable `reply`.

The method `withCRs` can be used to split the message across more than one line. The `\` sign is used to mark each point at which carriage return characters are to be placed.

```
Dialog warn: ('This is Dialog warn box\with its
    message split\across three lines') withCRs
```

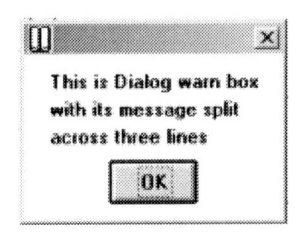

[Dialog box shown: "This is Dialog warn box with its message split across three lines" with OK button]

Dialog confirm
Dialog confrm boxes expect a boolean response from the user.

```
Dialog confirm: 'Is this a Dialog confirm box?'
```

[Dialog box shown: "Is this a Dialog confirm box?" with yes and no buttons]

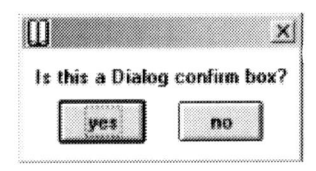

The answer returned is `true` if the **yes** button is clicked, and `false` if the **no** button is clicked.

```
(Dialog confirm: 'Do you have to be mad to work
                                            here?')
    ifTrue: [^'Yes you do have to be mad']
    ifFalse: [^'No you don't have to be mad but
                                        it helps']
```

or using a variable to reference the response;

```
reply:= Dialog confirm: 'Do you have to be mad to
                                work here?'.
(reply)
    ifTrue: [^'Yes you do have to be mad']
    ifFalse: [^'No you don't have to be mad but
                                        it helps']
```

65

Dialog request

Dialog request boxes expect a textual response from the user.

```
reply:=Dialog request: 'Please enter your age'
```

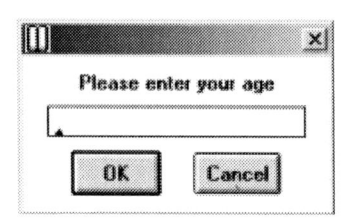

If an age is typed in and then, if the **OK** button is clicked, `reply` takes the value of whatever string has been typed.
If the **Cancel** button is pressed, `reply` references ' ', which is an empty string.
(Note that two single quotes represent an empty string; it is NOT a double quote.)

Using the `request: initialAnswer:` method, allows you to provide a default answer.

```
reply :=Dialog request: 'Please enter age'
         initialAnswer: '0'
```

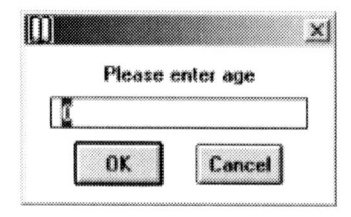

If the **OK** button is clicked, `reply` takes the value of whatever string is in the input box; ie the default, if nothing is typed.
If the **Cancel** button is pressed, `reply` references ' ' which is an empty string.

Using the `request: initialAnswer: onCancel:` method allows a meaningful answer to be returned, if the **Cancel** button is pressed.

```
reply := Dialog request: 'Please enter age'
          initialAnswer: '0'
          onCancel: ['Dialog has been cancelled']
```

In the above example, when the **OK** button is clicked, `reply` takes the value of whatever string is in the input box.
If the **Cancel** button is pressed, the `onCancel:` block code is executed, in this case making `reply` reference the string `'Dialog has been cancelled'`.

Note that when using dialog boxes, the input is always treated as a string, so when a number is required as in;

```
reply := Dialog request: 'Please enter your age'
               initialAnswer: '0'
```

and assuming the users enters `18`, the `reply` will reference the string `'18'`, not the integer. This cannot be used in arithmetic calculations, and before use it must be converted to a number. For example, as follows;

```
reply asNumber
```

Also see:
Association, Collection

Dictionary

Dictionary is a Smalltalk class. It is a kind of **Collection**.
See *Collection* for class hierarchy.

Objects of class **Association** can be placed in an instance of **Dictionary**.
An instance of **Dictionary** can hold any number of **Association** objects and will grow or shrink appropriately as elements are added or removed.
Dictionary objects are unordered.
Each **Association** instance in a dictionary consists of a *key-value* pair. Each *key* must be unique, although the same *value* may appear in any number of *key-value* pairings.
In principle the *keys* can be of any class but, in practice, they are most commonly **Integer**, **String** or **Symbol**.

Creation
You can create an instance of **Dictionary** by sending a `new` message to the **Dictionary** class.

67

The following statement creates an empty instance of **Dictonary**.

        myDictionary := Dictionary new

Adding elements
To add elements to a **Dictionary** instance, send an `add:` message. However, remember that the argument (ie the element to be added) must be an instance of **Association**.

        |myDictionary|
        myDictionary := Dictionary new.
        myDictionary add: (Association key: #emp1
                                      value: 'Peters').
        myDictionary add: (Association key: #emp2
                                      value: 'Smith').
        myDictionary add: (Association key: #emp3
                                      value: 'Patel')

The above program, creates an instance of **Dictionary** and adds three **Association** elements resulting in `myDictionary` referencing (`#emp1->'Peters' #emp2->'Smith' #emp3->'Patel'`), where the *keys* are the symbols; `#emp1`, `#emp2` and `#emp3`, and the *values* are the strings; `'Peters'`, `'Smith'` and `'Patel'`.

To add a value for an existing key, use the `at: aKey put: aValue` method.
This sets the value associated with `aKey` to `aValue`. If `aKey` is not found, it is added to the dictionary.

        myDictionary at: #emp2 put: 'Williams'.
        myDictionary at: #emp4 put: 'Ericson'

The above code will change the value associated with `#emp2` from `'Smith'` to `'Williams'` and insert a new association; `#emp4->'Ericson'`.

Retrieval
To retrieve an object from an instance of **Dictionary**, you can use the `at: aKey` method. This returns the value associated with the `aKey` argument. An error results if `aKey` cannot be found.

The following program creates and populates an instance of **Dictionary** and then returns the value associated with key; `#emp2`.

```
|myDictionary|
myDictionary := Dictionary new.
myDictionary add: (Association key: #emp1
                               value: 'Peters').
myDictionary add: (Association key: #emp2
                               value: 'Smith').
myDictionary add: (Association key: #emp3
                               value: 'Patel').
myDictionary at: #emp2
```

To retrieve an object from an instance of **Dictionary**, you can also use the `removeKey: aKey` method. This actually removes the association with the key `aKey` from the dictionary and returns the value of the association. Again, an error occurs if `aKey` cannot be found.

```
myDictionary removeKey: #emp2
```

The above statement removes the association `#emp2->'Smith'`, returning `'Smith'` as the answer.

Size
To determine the number of associations in a **Dictionary** object, send it the `size` message as follows.

```
myDictionary size
```

Iteration
To iterate over the elements in an instance of **Dictionary**, you can use a `do:` message. The following program creates an instance of **Dictionary** containing three employees, and then iterates through the contents adding each to a **SortedCollection**.

```
|myDictionary mySortedCollection|
mySortedCollection := SortedCollection new.
myDictionary := Dictionary new.
myDictionary at: #emp1 put: 'Peters'.
myDictionary at: #emp2 put: 'Williams'.
myDictionary at: #emp3 put: 'Patel'.
myDictionary at: #emp4 put: 'Ericson'.
myDictionary at: #emp5 put: 'Smith'.
myDictionary do: [:element |
                  mySortedCollection add: element]
```

The `keysAndValuesDo: aBlock` method iterates through an instance of **Dictionary**, with each of the receiver's *key-value* pairs as the block arguments. Assuming the variables `keySet` and `valueSet` have been declared, and `myDictionary` exists, the following code iterates through `myDictionary`, storing the keys in `keySet` and the values in `valueSet`.

```
keySet:=Set new.
valueSet:=Set new.
myDictionary keysAndValuesDo: [:key :value |
                               keySet add: key.
                               valueSet add: value]
```

Use
A **Dictionary** instance is an unordered collection of associations. Each **Association** instance consists of a *key-value* pair. The *key* provides a unique index to the corresponding *value*. A **Dictionary** object can be used to maintain an indexed list of objects where the list size and contents needs to be variable. A **Dictionary** object is somewhat similar to a simple two-column database table. This could be used, for example to list Product Codes (the *keys*) and corresponding Product Names (the *values*).

Difference

Also see:
Intersection, Set, Union

The difference between two sets is the set that contains all the elements of one set that are not elements of the other.

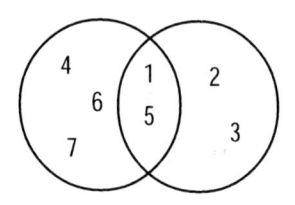

The following method answers the difference between two instances of class **Set**.
(Note that, if you wish to try this, it is safer to make it an instance method of your own subclass of **Set**, rather than modify the protocol of **Set**.)

```
difference: aSet to: newSet
"Finds the difference between aSet and the
receiver and stores the result in newSet.
Precondition: newSet must be empty.
Answers the receiver."
    ^(self - aSet) do: [:item | newSet add:
                                        item]
```

The following program creates three instances of **Set**. setA(1 4 5 6 7) and setB(1 2 3 5) are *differenced* to give the result in setC(4 6 7).

```
|setA setB setC|
setA := Set new.
setB := Set new.
setC := Set new.
setA add: 1; add: 4; add: 5; add: 6; add: 7.
setB add: 1; add: 2; add: 3; add: 5.
setA difference: setB to: setC
```

Also see:
Object-oriented programming

Encapsulation

This is a key principle in object-oriented thinking. It describes the situation where the data that represents the state of an object cannot be directly accessed from outside, but can only be accessed from other objects by using the methods provided.

To illustrate, consider a **BankAccount** object with the instance variable balance. Assume that the class defines the following instance methods.

```
balanceInPounds
"Answers the balance in £s"

credit100Pounds
"Credits the receiver account by £100"
```

When we have created a **BankAccount** object, other objects cannot get direct access to balance. The only way is by sending the **BankAccount** instance one of the messages defined by its two methods. Hence, all we can do with an instance of **BankAccount** is send it a `balanceInPounds` message to get the `balance` value, or send it a `credit100Pounds` message to increase the `balance` by £100. We have a simple and clearly defined interface to the class allowing us to get the balance or credit by £100. We can't do anything else at all unless new methods are defined as part of the **BankAccount** class. The bank account's data is encapsulated.

This has the great advantage that we can change internal data structures within objects without changing the code in the objects that communicate with them. Let's assume we want to store `balance` in French Francs instead of British Pounds. We can alter the **BankAccount** class as required and, providing we still have methods called; `balanceInPounds` and `credit100Pounds`, all objects that made use of these before are totally unaffected. This nicely limits the knock-on effects of any changes, making software maintenance much easier.

Errors

Also see:
Debugger

Programs can contain errors (or bugs). Good design and testing can improve our confidence that a piece of software is going to behave as required, but the fact remains that any moderately complex program is likely to contain some errors.

The easiest errors to deal with are those that are noticed by the compiler. Errors occurring at run-time will cause an 'exception to be raised'.

Some programming languages, including Smalltalk, provide mechanisms for 'trapping' errors, and they handle exceptions by executing some alternative code should an exception occur. This can ensure a smooth shutdown and avoid a computer 'crash'.

Programming environments usually provide 'debuggers', which are programs that aid the tracking down of errors. Among other things, they allow programs to be run one line at a time under user control, and variables can be checked while a program is executing.

Errors can be classified according to type;
- syntax errors
- semantic errors
- logical errors.

Syntax error
A syntax error occurs in a program when a program statement is not correctly constructed. This could be due to a spelling error or a mistake in punctuation.

"I am crathy." is an English syntax error because the sentence contains a spelling mistake.

The Smalltalk statement sequence;
```
myAge := 24
yourAge := myAge
```

contains a syntax error because the . statement separator is missing.

The compiler should spot syntax errors.

Semantic error
A semantic error occurs in a program when some aspect does not make sense, even though the syntax may be correct.

"The sky is three hours long." contains a semantic error because it makes no sense, even though there is no problem with the grammar.

For example, in Smalltalk, we could inadvertently assign a string object to a variable intended to reference a number. If we then try to use the string in a calculation, an error occurs.

In the following code, the variable age is assigned a string, which is then compared with the integer 65. Checking whether a string is greater than an integer makes no sense, even though the syntax is okay.

```
age := 'Eric'.
(if age > 65)
    ifTrue:[^'I am a pensioner']
```

Semantic errors will cause an exception when run.

Logical error
A logical error occurs in a program when the instructions provided by the code do not accomplish the intended purpose.

The statement; *"It is my birthday on Saturday. Today is Monday so tomorrow is my birthday."* is a natural language example of a logical error.

In the following Smalltalk program, the intention is to sum the numbers 0, 1, 2, 3 and 4.

```
|number sum|
number := 0.
sum:=0.
[number <4] whileTrue: [sum:=sum + number.
                        number:=number + 1].
^sum
```

The answer should be `10`, but `6` is returned because the condition block should be; `[number <=4]`.
This does not cause the program to raise an exception, it just gives the wrong result. Such errors are generally the most damaging in a program because they lead to incorrect results and can be difficult to find.

Expressions

Also see:
Messages

In Smalltalk, an expression can be an assignment, such as;
```
num1 := 3
```

which assigns the integer `3` to the variable named `num1`,

or a message-send, such as;
```
2 negated
```

which sends the message `negated` to the receiver, which is the integer `2`. The answer returned is `-2`.

Executable Smalltalk code consists of statements that are executed in sequence. Each statement consists of one or more expressions and statements are separated by a `.` (full-stop).

(Note that `.` is not used to terminate statements, but is used to separate them from one another. Therefore, it is not required after the final statement in a program. Neither is a `.` required immediately after the declaration of variables.)

When an object is sent a message, it always gives a reply. Therefore, wherever an object appears in an expression, you can substitute a message expression that gives a similar object as its answer.

For example, in the following message expression;
```
('Eric' size) + 3
```

`'Eric' size` answers the length of the receiver, which in this case is 4.

Thus the original expression now becomes;
```
4 + 3
```
which evaluates to 7.

Similarly, in the expression;
```
(8 * ('large' size)) + 2
```
the expression in the innermost parentheses is evaluated first. The answer is 5 as there are five characters in the string `'large'`.
This now gives an expression;
```
(8 * 5) + 2
```
Next; `8 * 5` answers 40, so we get;
```
40 + 2
```
which answers 42.

In the expression;
```
myAccount credit: (6 * 100)
```
the message expression `6 * 100` is evaluated first, answering 600, which becomes the argument used in the `credit:` message, as in;
```
myAccount credit: 600
```

A cascaded message provides a shorthand way of writing a sequence of messages that are all being sent to the same receiver.
The receiver only needs to be stated once and is followed by the sequence of messages separated from one another using ; (semi-colon).
For example, the following expression series puts numbers into an instance of **Set** called mySet;

```
mySet add: 4.
mySet add: 6.
mySet add: 8
```

and can be rewritten as a cascaded message;
```
mySet add: 4; add: 6; add: 8
```

75

Files

Also see:
Streams

The class **Filename** enables us to connect to the disk filing system.

There are two main ways to create an instance of **Filename**. We can either create an instance directly using `named:` or convert a string using `asFilename`.

```
myFile := Filename named: 'c:\test.txt'.
myFile := 'c:\test.txt' asFilename
```

The class provides a number of instance methods including;

```
myFile directory.    "answers a FATFilename('c:\')"
myFile head.         "answers 'c:\' "
myFile tail          "answers 'test.txt'   "
```

We can access a file by creating a stream on the file. The following messages are amongst those that can be used;

`readStream`   "Opens an existing file to be read."

`writeStream`   "Opens a file for writing. If the file does not already exist, it will be created. If it does exist, the contents will be deleted."

`appendStream`   "Opens a file to be appended. If the file does not already exist, it will be created. Writing is to the end of the file."

`readWriteStream` "Opens a file for reading and writing. If the file does not already exist, it will be created. If it does exist, the contents are not deleted. The read/write position can be anywhere in the stream."

Read can always be at any position in the stream, whereas write is often only to the end of the file.

Message	Read	Write	Creates file	Deletes content
readStream	yes	no	no	no
writeStream	no	yes (end of file)	yes	yes
appendStream	no	yes (end of file)	yes	no
readWriteStream	yes	yes (any position)	yes	no

When a file is finished with, it must be closed. This is achieved by sending it a `close` message.

The following program creates a file called `test.txt` on the `C` drive and writes to it; `'Hello everybody'`.

```
|file stream|
file:=Filename named: 'c:\test.txt'.
stream:= file writeStream.
stream nextPutAll:'Hello everybody'.
stream close
```

The file now contains;
```
Hello everybody
```

Now that the file exists we can add to the end of it using `appendStream`.

```
file:=Filename named: 'c:\test.txt'.
stream:= file appendStream.
stream cr; nextPutAll: 'How ya doing?'.
stream close
```

So the file now contains;
```
Hello everybody
How ya doing?
```

To read the file, we could use `readStream`. In this example, we output the text to a **Dialog** box.

```
file:=Filename named: 'c:\test.txt'.
stream:= file readStream.
text := stream contents.
stream close.
Dialog warn: text
```

77

Float

Also see:
Fraction, Integer, Number, Rounding

The class **Float** defines the protocol for operations on floating-point numbers. See *Number* for class hierarchy.

Instances of class **Float** are floating-point numbers.
For example;
```
3.142
-0.786
3.8e2          "Meaning 3.8 x 10², which is 380"
```

Fraction

Also see:
Float, Integer, Number

The class **Fraction** defines the protocol for operations on rational numbers. See *Number* for class hierarchy.

Instances of class **Fraction** represent rational numbers. Fractions are created when an integer is sent a / (divide) message with an integer argument, and the answer does not give an integer result.
For example;
```
(2 / 3)
(22 / 7)
```

Garbage collection

Also see:
Scope, Variables

Garbage collection describes the process of reclaiming memory that is no longer used by a program. Some programming languages require the programmer to explicitly take care of memory resource allocation and subsequent deallocation. However, Smalltalk environments look after garbage collection automatically.

Objects that are no longer referenced are garbage collected, freeing the memory space that they occupy. This will occur, for example, when an object's only variable reference goes out of scope, or is made to reference a different object.

Variables provide references to objects, and a single object can be referenced by more than one variable. In the following diagram, the variables `myName` and `myUnclesName` both reference the same object.

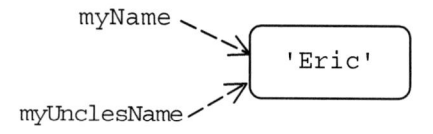

```
     myName ╲
              ╲→ ┌─────────┐
                 │ 'Eric'  │
              ╱→ └─────────┘
myUnclesName ╱
```

If both variable names are removed, we still have the object in memory, but it is lost because we have no way of referencing it. Garbage collection will free the space occupied by the object that is no longer referenced.

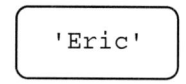

```
┌─────────┐
│ 'Eric'  │
└─────────┘
```

Automatic garbage collection is convenient but does add some subtle unpredictability to run times. This is because we cannot predict exactly when garbage collection will take place and, when it does, it occupies processor time. A disadvantage of giving the programmer the responsibility for garbage collection is that, if deallocation is not done correctly, memory can fill up with unreferenced objects, reducing the amount of available free memory. This is called 'memory leak', and is sometimes a source of hard to track bugs.

Also see:
Local variable, Temporary variable, Scope, Variables

Global variable

Global variables allow you to have objects that can be used throughout your system. They are defined in dictionaries called pool dictionaries. Global variable names, and the values that they reference, are linked together through **Association** instances in the dictionary.

Global variable names follow the same naming rules as for other variables, except they should always begin with a capital letter.

All the class names and global variables needed by your system are stored in a special pool dictionary called the system dictionary, which is referenced by the name `Smalltalk`.

To check the version of Smalltalk you are using, send the Smalltalk dictionary the message; `version`.

```
Smalltalk version
```

It should answer something like;

`'VisualWorks(R), Release 2.5.2 of September 26, 1995'`

The message expression;
```
Smalltalk at: #Age put: 30
```

creates a global variable `Age` with value `30`.

However, it is better not to clutter up the `Smalltalk` dictionary with your own global variables.

The class **PoolDictionary** is a subclass of **Dictionary** and, although the system dictionary is predefined for you and can be accessed by all classes, you can define your own pool dictionary of global variables that can be accessed just by the classes you specify.

You can use the *Class browser* to create a new instance of **PoolDictionary**, or in the *Workspace* execute the following message expression.

```
Smalltalk at: #MyPoolDictionary put:
                         Dictionary new
```

Adding `MyPoolDictionary` to the `Smalltalk` dictionary makes it universally known.

Whenever class variables are created they are put into a pool dictionary for the class. The protocol for accessing pool dictionaries is inherited by all classes from the class; **Class**.

Classes that want to access the objects in `MyPoolDictionary` have to register an interest.

The following expression, evaluated in the *Workspace*, creates a subclass of **Object** called **Car** with instance variables `make` and `colour`. It is given no class variables and its pool dictionary is set to be `MyPoolDictionary`.

```
Object subclass: #Car
instanceVariableNames: 'make colour'
classVariableNames: ''
poolDictionaries: 'MyPoolDictionary'
```

Alternatively, classes that have already been defined can register `MyPoolDictionary` in their class definition.

```
Car addSharedPool: MyPoolDictionary
```

Objects to be shared can be added to `MyPoolDictionary`.
The following expression sets up a global variable called `Name`, with its value set to `'Eric'`.

```
MyPoolDictionary at: #Name put: 'Eric'
```

Methods defined in the **Car** class now all have access to the `Name` variable. In similar fashion, other classes could register access to this pool dictionary.

(Note that, although global variables are sometimes necessary, it is generally not a good idea to use global variables in your programming as these circumvent the principles of encapsulation.)

Inheritance

Also see:
Object-oriented programming

The concept of inheritance is key feature of object-oriented programming. Inheritance means that a class can be created as a subclass of another and thereby take on its attributes and behaviour. This can save us a lot of work. For example, assume we have a class **Person**, which implements the attributes and behaviour we want from **Person** objects. For a business application we could create a subclass called **Employee** or, for a university system, a subclass **Student**.

The diagram on the following page shows this class hierarchy.

```
         ┌─────────────┐
         │   Person    │
         └─────────────┘
            ▲       ▲
           ╱         ╲
┌─────────────┐   ┌─────────────┐
│  Employee   │   │   Student   │
└─────────────┘   └─────────────┘
```

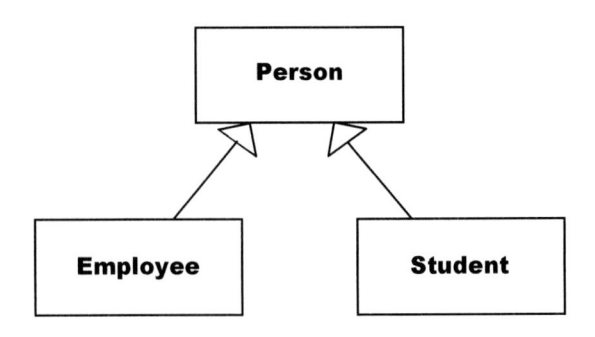

Both of these subclasses would inherit the attributes and behaviour of the **Person** class, saving us the job of writing new methods to handle common tasks such as setting `name` or `age`. Our subclasses would inherit all the attributes and all the behaviour defined by **Person**. The concept is similar to genetic inheritance. (Thanks to my mother I have a large nose, and my wife often tells me; *"You sound just like your father"*.)

However, the subclasses can add new attributes and behaviours of their own, thus extending the capabilities of the parent class. (I do my own plumbing, which neither of my parents did!)

The new classes can also override an inherited behaviour to do something different when sent the same message. For example, our **Student** class could inherit a print behaviour from **Person**, but override this with its own `print` method to print the extra details that a **Student** has, such as course name, year, etc. (My children are better at football than I am, so they have managed to override any inherited method of kicking a ball.)

Inheritance isn't limited to the direct parent (or superclass) of a class but is passed down from the superclass of the superclass, and so on. The 'mother' of all Smalltalk classes being the root class called **Object**.

Inspector

Also see:
Class browser, Debugger, Workspace

The *Inspector* is a tool provided within the Smalltalk development environment allowing you to display the attributes of an object and their current values.

An *Inspector* window can be opened by using the interactive tools provided by your system or by sending an object the `inspect` message.

Evaluating the expression;
```
    myCar inspect
```
opens a window something like the following.

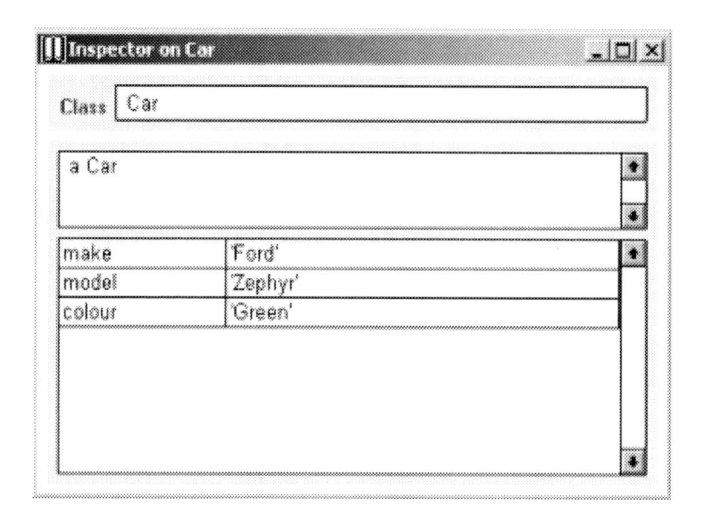

```
┌─ Inspector on Car ──────────────── _ □ × ┐
│  Class │ Car                            │
│        ┌─────────────────────────────┐  │
│        │ a Car                       │  │
│        │                             │  │
│        ├──────┬──────────────────────┤  │
│        │ make │ 'Ford'                │  │
│        │ model│ 'Zephyr'              │  │
│        │ colour│ 'Green'              │  │
│        │                             │  │
│        └─────────────────────────────┘  │
└─────────────────────────────────────────┘
```

Also see:
  Class, Methods, Variables

Instance creation

The principal way of creating an instance of a class is to send the class the message new.

    mySet := Set new.

creates an empty set, Set (), and assigns this instance of **Set** to the variable mySet.

When creating fixed-size collections we can specify the required size using a new: message.

    myArray := Array new: 5.

creates an **Array** instance #(nil nil nil nil nil) with five empty object refences.

`new` and `new:` are implemented in the **Behavior** class, although they may be overridden.

Some objects can be created automatically without having to explicitly send a `new` message.

For example, **Number** objects;
```
    myInteger := 67
    myFloat   := 3.142
```

String objects;
```
    myString := 'Eric'
```

Character objects;
```
    myCharacter := $A
```

Symbol objects;
```
    mySymbol := #menu
```

Array objects;
```
    myArray := #(3 5 6)
```

Point objects;
```
    myPoint := 6 @ 12
```

Association objects;
```
    myAssociation := 56 -> 'Anita'
```

BlockClosure objects;
```
    myBlock := [42 printString]
```

The following shows how to create instances of a class that we have defined ourselves.

Assume we wish to define a class **Car** with attributes make and colour. We can subclass **Car** from **Object** and define instance variables `make` and `colour`. The accessor methods for these instance variables are:

```
    make
    "Getter method for the make attribute.  Answers
    the value of make"
         ^ make
```

```
make: aMake
    "Setter method for the make attribute.  Answers
    receiver"
        make := aMake

colour
    "Getter method for the colour attribute.  Answers
    the value of colour"
        ^ colour

colour: aColour
    "Setter method for the colour attribute.  Answers
    receiver"
        colour := aColour
```

Once we have defined the **Car** class, with its instance variables and instance methods, we can create an instance of **Car**.
In the *Workspace*, this is achieved by executing the statement;
```
    myCar := Car new
```

We can use the *Inspector* by sending `myCar` an `inspect` message;
```
    myCar inspect
```

(Or by selecting `myCar` and using the interface **Inspect** option) to open an *Inspector* window on `myCar`.

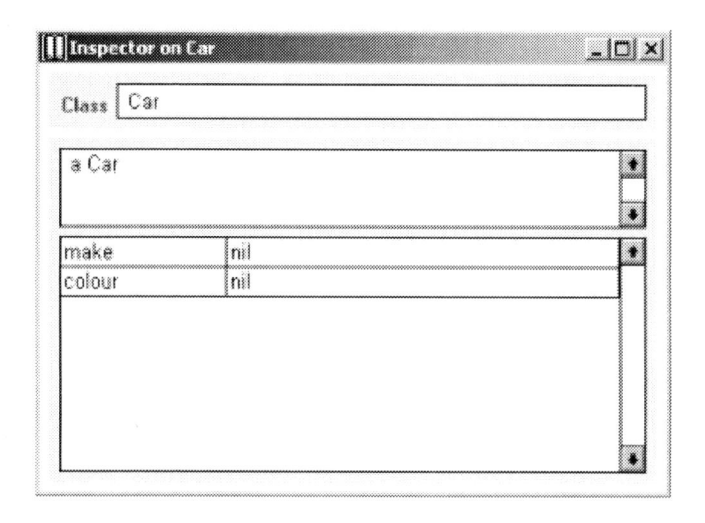

Class	Car
a Car	

make	nil
colour	nil

As you can see, the instance has been created and has had its instance variables set to `nil`.

(Note that we have not defined a `new` method for the **Car** class, so it simply uses the inherited method.)

We could write another instance method called `initialize` to initialise the values of `make` and `colour`.

```
initialize
"Initializes an instance of Car.
make is set to 'Ford'
colour is set to 'Black'
Answers the receiver"
    self make: 'Ford'.
    self colour: 'Black'
```

Hence executing;
    `myCar initialize`

in the *Workspace* and inspecting, gives;

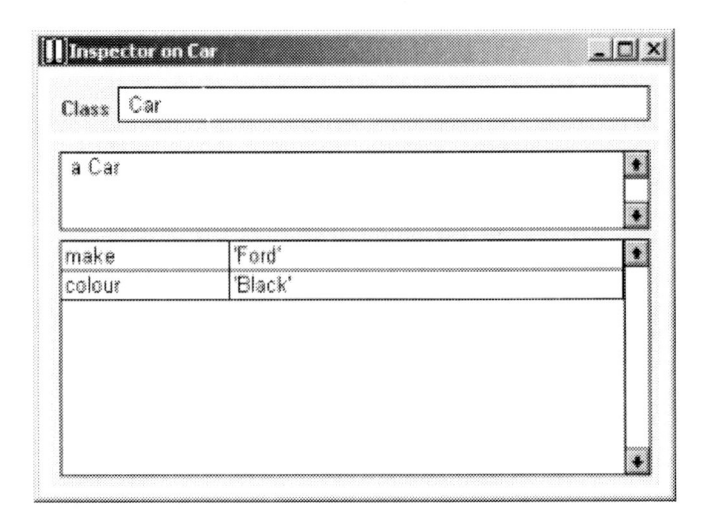

If we wish to create a new instance of **Car** with initialised variables we can now type in the *Workspace*;
    `myCar := Car new initialize`

Alternatively we can override the inherited `new` method by defining a class method called `new` within the class **Car**.

```
new
    "Class method to create a new instance of Car and
    initialize it."
    ^ super new initialize
```

Now executing the statement;
```
    myCar := Car new.
```

uses **Car**'s own `new` method rather than the inherited method. Within **Car**'s `new` method, the message expression `super new` causes the search for the `new` method to start in the superclass of the receiver. This search will find the original `new` method and create a new instance of **Car**. This newly minted instance is then sent the message `initialize`, which is found in class **Car**. This initialises the new instance. This instance of **Car** is the object given in answer, thanks to the `^` symbol.

Be careful that you don't implement `new` as follows.

```
new
    "INCORRECT Class method to create a new instance
    of Car and initialize it.
    Answers the new initialized Car instance"
    ^ self new initialize
```

When this method is executed, `self new` causes the search for `new` to begin in the **Car** class. It therefore finds this same `new` method and runs it. This, in turn, does the same thing again until the execution stack fills and your system locks up in a recursive loop. See *Recursion*.
Also, look what happens if you miss out the `^`.

```
new
    "INCORRECT Class method to create a new instance
    of Car and initialize it."
        super new initialize
```

Then, in the *Workspace*;
```
    myCar := Car new
```
creates a new, correctly initialized instance of **Car**, but the `new` method does not give this object as its answer. Instead, by default, it answers the receiver.

87

The receiver of the new message is the class **Car**, so it is the class itself that is returned rather than the instance and, when we inspect myCar, it is not what we wanted.

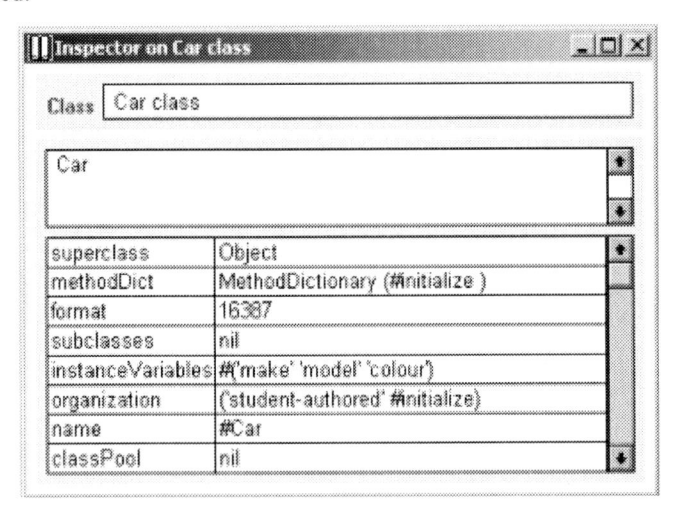

Inspector on Car class	_ □ ×

Class	Car class

Car

superclass	Object
methodDict	MethodDictionary (#initialize)
format	16387
subclasses	nil
instanceVariables	#('make' 'model' 'colour')
organization	('student-authored' #initialize)
name	#Car
classPool	nil

Instance method

Also see:
Accessor method, Class method, Messages, Methods

When an object is sent a message, it is expected to respond by carrying out the associated behaviour. Instance methods implement this behaviour by defining the code to be executed when a message is sent to an instance of a class.

Assume that we have a class **Person** that has a name attribute. The class definition would include an instance variable to store this attribute value and every instance of **Person** that we create will be an individual object with its own name variable. The required behaviours will be implemented as methods.

Therefore, to set the value referenced by name, the **Person** class must have a method called name: defined as part of its protocol.

The method to set the name of a **Person** instance would be;

> `name: aString`
> `"Sets the name instance variable of the receiver`
> `to the value referenced by aString.`
> `Answers the receiver."`
>   `name := aString`

So when the message `name: 'Anita'` is sent to an instance of **Person**;
    `aPerson   name: 'Anita'`

execution passes to the `name:` method, which assigns the string `'Anita'` (referenced by the parameter `aString` within the method) to the instance variable `name`.

Also see:
   Class variable, Class instance variable,
   Variables

Instance variable

Instance variables are used to represent the attributes of an object.
By convention, instance variable names begin with a lowercase letter.

For example, the class **Person** may have attributes, name, age and gender. These attributes could be represented respectively by instance variables called; name, age and gender.
When an instance of **Person** has been created, we can assign values to these variables. So called *setter methods* are employed for this purpose.

The following expression series creates a new instance of **Person**, assigns it to a variable called `eldestSon`, and then sets its attribute values using the setter methods.

> `|eldestSon|`
> `eldestSon := Person new.`
> `eldestSon name: 'Andrew'.`
> `eldestSon age: 24.`
> `eldestSon gender: 'male'`

Instance variables can only be accessed by the methods of the class in which they are declared, or by its subclasses through inheritance.

> **Integer**

Also see:
Float, Fraction, Number, Rounding

The class **Integer** is an abstract class that defines the common protocol for operations on whole numbers.
See *Number* for class hierarchy.

Integer objects can be positive or negative whole numbers.

Instances of **SmallInteger** are in the range −16,384 to 16,383.

Instances of **LargePositiveInteger** and **LargeNegativeInteger** are larger positive and negative integers.

The different classes reflect the fact that internal storage of integers differs depending on size and sign, and are designed to ensure efficient processing speed and memory demands.

−536870912 to 536870911

> **Interpreted language**

Also see:
Bytecode, Compiled language

Machine code is the program code that can be executed directly on a computer's processor. The instructions written using a high-level language are called source code. So that the computer's processor can run them, programs written in high-level languages must be converted from the original source code into machine code.
Interpreted languages are high-level programming languages that are converted to machine code on a line-by-line basis as they are run. The conversion from source code is carried out using a program called an Interpreter. This is in contrast to compiled languages, which are fully translated as a distinct process before execution.

The disadvantage of interpreted languages is that execution is likely to be slower than for compiled languages.
The main advantage is that programs can seem easier to debug as you do not have to wait for them to compile.

Also see:
Difference, Set, Union

Intersection

The intersection of two sets is the set that contains the elements that belong to both sets.

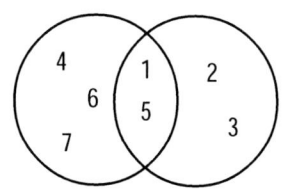

The following method answers the intersection of two instances of class **Set**.

```
intersection: aSet to: newSet
"Finds the intersection of aSet and the receiver
and stores the result in newSet.
Precondition: newSet must be empty
Answers the receiver."

    (self - (self - aSet)) do: [:item |
                        newSet add: item]
```

The following program creates three instances of **Set**. setA (1 4 5 6 7) and setB (1 2 3 5) are *intersected* to give the result in setC (1 5).

```
|setA setB setC|
setA := Set new.
setB := Set new.
setC := Set new.
setA add: 1; add: 4; add: 5; add: 6; add: 7.
setB add: 1; add: 2; add: 3; add: 5.
setA intersection: setB to: setC
```

(Note that, if you wish to try this, it is safer to make it an instance method of your own subclass of **Set**, rather than modify the protocol of **Set**.)

91

Iteration

Also see:
Conditional expressions

Iteration is the process of repeating some action a number of times.

A computer program that is required to do anything repeatedly must know when to stop. This could be;

- after a set number of times,
- when a true or false condition is met,
- when some other specified value is reached.

Smalltalk provides the following keyword selectors to handle iteration. These are;

```
timesRepeat:
whileTrue:
whileFalse:
to:do:
do:
```

timesRepeat:
This requires an integer as its receiver and a code block as its argument. The code block is evaluated repeatedly, the number of times specified by the integer receiver.

For example, the following program increments `count` on each iteration before returning its final value; 3.

```
|count|
count:=0.
3 timesRepeat: [count := count + 1].
^count
```

whileTrue:
This requires a boolean condition block as its receiver and a code block as its argument.
Before each iteration, the boolean condition block is evaluated. If it evaluates to `true`, the argument code block is evaluated. This repeats for as long as the boolean condition block receiver remains `true`.

The following program increments `count` repeatedly while `count<4`. On the fourth iteration, `count` is set to 4, and the boolean expression `count<4` evaluates to `false`, so the looping ends and the value 4 is returned.

```
|count|
count:=0.
[count<4] whileTrue: [count:=count + 1].
^count
```

whileFalse:
This requires a boolean condition block as its receiver and a code block as its argument.

Before each iteration, the boolean condition block is evaluated. If it evaluates to `false`, the argument code block is evaluated. This repeats for as long as the boolean condition block receiver remains `false`.

This program decrements `count` repeatedly while `count<0`. On the fourth iteration, `count` will have reached 0, but the boolean expression `count<0` still evaluates to `false`, so the looping continues one more time, giving a return `count` value of -1.

```
|count|
count:=4.
[count<0] whileFalse: [count:=count - 1].
^count
```

Care must be taken to ensure that the loop terminating condition will be reached. In a `whileTrue:` loop, if the boolean condition block never becomes `false`, the loop will never end and your program will crash.
Similarly, a crash will occur if the boolean condition block in a `whileFalse:` loop never becomes `true`.

The argument code block MUST do something that alters a value in the boolean condition block or nothing within the loop can possibly ensure that the loop ever ends.

to: do:
This keyword selector requires an integer as its receiver, and as its first argument, with a code block as its second argument. The receiver and first argument define a start and stop value, and the code block specifies what is to be done at each iteration.

93

```
|count|
count:=0.
2 to: 5 do: [:index | count := count + index].
^count
```

In the above program, the code block is repeatedly evaluated with index taking the values 2, 3, 4 and 5 for each of the three iterations as defined by the receiver 2 and the argument 5.

Number of Iteration	index value	count value
1	2	2
2	3	5
3	4	9
4	5	14

Thus the value of count returned is 14.

do:
do: iterates through each of the elements in the receiver.

The following program counts the number of lowercase letters in the string 'The Quick Brown Fox'.

```
|littleLetterCount|
littleLetterCount := 0.
'The Quick Brown Fox' do:
        [:char | char isLowercase
             ifTrue: [
                 littleLetterCount :=
                      littleLetterCount + 1]].
^littleLetterCount
```

Other useful methods for iteration include select: and reject:.

select:
Iterates through each of the elements in the receiver and answers all the elements for which the argument block evaluates to true.

```
^('the quick brown fox' select: [:char |
                        char isVowel] ) size
```
The above answers 5, which is the number of vowels in the receiver string.

reject:
Iterates through each of the elements in the receiver and answers all the elements for which the argument block evaluates to `false`.

```
^('the quick brown fox' reject: [:char |
                            char isVowel] ) size
```
The above answers `14`, which is the number of consonants in the receiver string.

Also see:
Binary message, Messages, Unary message

Keyword message

A keyword message consists of one or more keywords to make up the message selector. Each keyword ends in a `:` and must be followed by an argument. In the expression;

```
myFridge temperature: 4
```

the receiver is the object instance `myFridge`, the message selector is `temperature:` and the argument is `4`. The message sent to the object `myFridge` is `temperature: 4`, which is a keyword message.

Similarly, in the following expression;

```
5 plus: 2
```

the receiver is `5`, the message selector is `plus:` and the argument is `2`. `plus: 2` is the keyword message.
(Note that it is important you do not put a space between the keyword and `:`. If you do, an error will occur.)

Some keyword messages need more than one argument and thus require more than one keyword. For example the expression;

```
yourAccount transfer: 500   to: myAccount
```

contains the keyword message; `transfer: 500 to: myAccount`. The receiver is `yourAccount`. The first keyword; `transfer:` and the second keyword; `to:` each have an argument; in this case; `500` and `myAccount` respectively. `transfer:to:` is the message selector.

> **Literals**

Also see:
Array, Character, Float, Fraction, Integer, Number, String, Symbol

Smalltalk provides five basic, or literal classes.

These are; **Number**, **Character**, **String**, **Symbol** and **Array**.

Number
Number is actually subclassed as **Integer**, **Float** and **Fraction**, so a **Number** instance can be an integer, a floating-point number or a fraction.

Integer
An integer is any whole number, positive or negative, including 0.
For example;
    42
    -42
    0

Float
A floating-point number is any real number with a decimal part.
For example;
    3.142
    -3.142
    2.0
    0.004
    -7.13e2

(Note that -7.13e2 represents –7.13 exponential 2, which is –7.13 x 10^2, which is -713.0.)

A floating-point number, including any exponent, should not be written to begin or end with a decimal point.

Therefore, the following are not allowed.

    .564
    39.
    5.6e.2

Fraction
A fraction is a rational number and can be negative or positive.
For example;
   2/3
   -1/9

Character
An instance of **Character** can be any ASCII character and is written with a $ prefix.
For example;
   $A   denotes the character A and;
   $&   denotes the character &.

Symbol
Variable name identifiers and message selectors are instances of **Symbol** and are written with a # prefix.
For example;
   #*   is a binary message selector
   #do: is a keyword message selector
   #address   is an identifier or variable name.

Array
An instance of **Array** is a data structure containing an array of elements, each of which can be any class of object. A literal array is an indexed list of literals. The list is enclosed in parentheses and prefixed with a hash; #.
For example;
   #(1 2 3 4)   produces an array of four integers, and;
   #(4 $A 'Eric')   produces an array of three elements; an integer, a character and a string.

String
An instance of **String** (or more accurately of **ByteString**) is a sequence of characters and is written within single quotes.

The following represent string objects.

   'This is a string'
   'Eric is a &#%£'

Local variable

Also see:
Assignment, Global variable, Scope, Temporary variable, Variables

A variable is a name used to refer to an object. The object referred to is said to be the variable's value. Variables are made to refer to a value by assignment.

Local variables are declared in a method by listing them between vertical bars.

```
calculateCelsius
    "Assumes the receiver is a number representing a
    temperature in degrees Fahrenheit.
    Answers the corresponding temperature in degrees
    Celsius"

    |fahrenheit  celsius|

    fahrenheit := self.
    celsius : = (fahrenheit - 32 ) * 5 / 9.
    ^celsius
```

In the above method, fahrenheit and celsius are declared as local variables. (Note that no . is required to separate the declaration from the program statement that follows it.) They are called local because they are only known to the method in which they appear. In fact, we say that their scope is limited to this method. They come into existence when the method is run and cease existence afterwards. This means that we can have other methods, with local variables that use the same names, without any possibility of confusion.

Local variables are sometimes also called temporary variables, and normally there is no distinction between them. However, in the LearningWorks™ environment, a distinction is made.

The term temporary variable is used to describe variables declared within vertical bars inside methods or in the *Workspace*.

The term local variable is used to describe variables that are declared by clicking the **Create it** button after attempting to evaluate in the *Workspace*.

Also see:
   Boolean, Conditional expressions   **Logical operators**

Two objects can be compared with one another using any of the following binary message selectors. The result of any comparison will be either `true` or `false`. The objects must be comparable objects such as numbers, characters, strings or symbols. In fact, we can compare any objects derived from the **Magnitude** class.

`>`	Answers `true` if the receiver is greater than the argument, otherwise `false`.
`<`	Answers `true` if the receiver is less than the argument, otherwise `false`.
`>=`	Answers `true` if the receiver is greater than or equal to the argument, otherwise `false`.
`<=`	Answers `true` if the receiver is less than or equal to the argument, otherwise `false`.
`=`	Answers `true` if the receiver is equal in value to the argument, otherwise `false`.
`~=`	Answers `true` if the receiver is not equal in value to the argument, otherwise `false`.
`==`	Answers `true` if the receiver is the same object as the argument, otherwise `false`.
`~~`	Answers `true` if the receiver is not the same object as the argument, otherwise `false`.

In the following message expressions;

```
6 > 9      "evaluates to false because 6 is NOT greater than 9"
6 < 9      "evaluates to true because 6 IS less than 9"
4 >= 3     "evaluates to true because 4 IS greater than 3"
3 <= 3     "evaluates to true because 3 IS equal in value to 3"
6 = 6      "evaluates to true because 6 IS equal in value to 6"
6 ~= 6     "evaluates to false because it is not true that 6 is not equal
            in value to 6"
6 == 6     "evaluates to true because 6 is actually the identical object
            to 6"
6 ~~ 6     "evaluates to false because 6 is the identical object to 6"
```

'Eric' = 'Eric' evaluates to `true` because the strings have the same value.
However, `'Eric'=='Eric'` evaluates to `false` because, although the strings have the same value, they are NOT the same object. We actually have two strings and both just happen to have the same value.

Consider the program;

```
|name1 name2|
name1:='Eric'.
name2:=name1.
^(name1==name2)
```

The return value is `true` because `name1` and `name2` reference the same string.

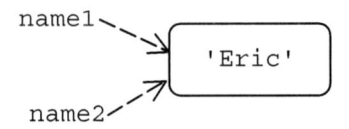

```
name1 ─┐
       ├─→ 'Eric'
name2 ─┘
```

However in;

```
|name1 name2|
name1:='Eric'.
name2:='Eric'.
^(name1==name2)
```

The return value is `false` because `name1` and `name2` reference separate instances of **ByteString** that both happen to have the same value.

```
name1 ──→ 'Eric'        name2 ──→ 'Eric'
```

`#Eric==#Eric` always evaluates to `true` because instances of **Symbol** are unique and only one **Symbol** can exist with any given value.

Methods that answer `true` or `false` are called predicates.
Besides those discussed above, Smalltalk also provides predicates for testing whether an object belongs to a particular class.

isInteger
The message `isInteger` answers `true` if the receiver is an instance of **Integer**, otherwise `false`.
For example;
```
64 isInteger            "answers true"
'Peter' isInteger       "answers false"
```

isString
`isString` answers `true` if the receiver is an instance of **ByteString**, otherwise `false`.
For example;
```
64 isString             "answers false"
'Peter' isString        "answers true"
```

To check whether a **Collection** object is empty of elements, `isEmpty` answers `true` if the receiver is an empty collection.

For example;
```
mySet := Set new.
mySet isEmpty           "answers true"
```

There are other possible methods used for comparison, such as;
```
min:
max:
between: and:
|
&
or:
and:
```

For example;
```
6 max: 3                "answers the receiver or the argument,
                         whichever has the greatest magnitude.
                         In this case 6"
3 between: 1 and: 9     "answers true"
```

But be careful as;
```
3 between: 9 and: 1
```
answers `false` because the method; `between aMin and: aMax` only answers `true` if the receiver is less than or equal to `aMax` and greater than or equal to `aMin`.

101

Magnitude

Also see:
Character, Date, Logical operators, Number, Time

Magnitude is an abstract class.

Class hierarchy:

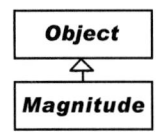

```
    Object
      △
  Magnitude
```

It provides the common comparing and ordering protocol inherited by its subclasses.
The subclasses of **Magnitude** define objects that can be compared, measured and ordered. They include numbers, characters, dates and times.

Messages

Also see:
Binary/Keyword/Unary message, Expressions, Methods, Precedence

Objects can have behaviour (ie they can carry out actions). This only happens when they receive a message from another object, or from the user.

A simple message expression is written in the form;
>   *object message*

where *object* is the object receiving the message, and *message* is the message. Sending a message to an object can cause it to provide information about itself, change its state, or carry out some other action including sending messages to other objects.

In the message expression;
>   `4 negated`

`4` is the receiver and `negated` is the message.
When a message is sent to an object it always gives a reply. In this case the answer is the integer −4.

Sending a message to an object only works if the object has been designed to 'understand' that message. The message must be part of the object's protocol. (That is, in the list of messages the object understands.)

My dog responds to the following message protocol;
```
sit
lay-down
biccy
din-din
walkies
```

Send him any other message and he will ignore it and just look dopey.

When an object receives a message, Smalltalk looks for the message name amongst the methods defined for the object's class. If it finds a match, it executes the code in the corresponding method, otherwise it looks for a matching method in the direct superclass of the object's class. If necessary it will then search the superclass's superclass until a matching method is found. If the top of the class hierarchy (ie **Object** class) is reached, and no method has been found, an error occurs. See *Inheritance*.

A message selector is the symbol used to name a message in Smalltalk.

There are three types of message selector, each corresponding to one of the three types of message; Unary, Binary and Keyword.

A unary message selector forms a message on its own, because unary messages take no arguments.

For example, in the expression;
```
5 negated
```
the receiver is `5` and the message selector is `negated`.

A binary message selector followed by an argument forms a binary message.

For example, `+` is a binary message selector used for arithmetic addition.

In the expression;
```
4 + 6
```

`4` is the receiver, `+` the binary message selector, and `+ 6` is the message.

103

A keyword message selector, with one or more arguments, forms a keyword message.

For example;
    `plus:` is a keyword selector used for arithmetic addition.

In the expression;
    `4 plus: 6`

4 is the receiver, `plus:` the keyword message selector, and `plus: 6` is the message.

Keyword selectors may take more than one argument. For example in the expression;
    `myAccount transfer: 350 to: yourAccount`

the receiver is `myAccount`, and the message is `transfer: 350 to: yourAccount`. The keyword message selector is `transfer:to:`.

Because the answer given to a sent message is always an object, message-sending expressions can be strung together in a series, sometimes called a chain.

In the following example;
    `-5.6 negated rounded`

Smalltalk evaluates the messages from left to right so that the receiver object, ie the instance of **Float**, `-5.6`, is first sent the message `negated`. This answers another instance of **Float**, `5.6`, making the expression effectively become;
    `5.6 rounded`.

The receiver object is now `5.6` which is sent the message `rounded`, which rounds the floating point number to its nearest integer, thus answering the **SmallInteger** object; `6`.

The order of evaluation of chained messages is in accordance with Smalltalk's rules of Precedence.

104

Also see:
Class, Class hierarchy

Metaclass

The objects in a Smalltalk program are instances of classes. If we create a new instance of a class, it gets all of its attributes and behaviour from the instance variables and instance methods defined by the class. So, if we create an instance of a **Frog** class;

```
kermit : = Frog new
```

`kermit` is endowed with all the attributes and behaviours of a **Frog** object.

But what about when we create a new class? Where do the behaviours we expect of a class come from?

One of the required behaviours is to respond to a `new` message. When we create a new class, we create new instances without necessarily writing a class method to implement the message `new`. Classes inherit the class method `new` so you would expect to find it in the class **Object**. But it's not there!

The fact is that classes are themselves objects. That is, each class is itself an instance of a class.

Try sending the class **Set** the message `class`;

```
Set class
```

The answer is `Set class`. So **Set** is an instance of **Set class**.

But then what class is **Set class** an instance of?

Check it out with;
```
Set class class
```

You will find that the answer is `Metaclass`.

The **Metaclass** describes the class variables and class methods for the class. Thus, **Set class** is the **Metaclass** instance, of which the **Set** class is itself an instance. Whenever a class is created, Smalltalk creates a corresponding instance of **Metaclass**. Thus a parallel hierarchy is maintained between classes and metaclasses.

Evaluating the expression;

```
Metaclass superclass
```

shows that **Metaclass** inherits from a class called **ClassDescription**.

And the expression;

```
ClassDescription superclass
```

shows that **ClassDescription** inherits from **Behavior**, which is in fact where behaviours such as `new` are implemented.

The superclass of **Behavior** is **Object**.

At the top of the hierarchy, the class **Object** is itself an instance of the metaclass **Object class**.

Hence, the expression;

```
Object class
```

answers **Object class**.

If we check the superclass of **Object class**;

```
Object class superclass
```

we find that **Object class** inherits from **Class** and;

```
Class superclass
```

shows that like **Metaclass**, **Class** is a subclass of **ClassDescription**.

The diagram on the following page shows the class hierarhy for **Set**.
The two types of arrow show where a class is a subclass of another, and which classes are instances of which other classes.
The diagram also shows an instance of **Set** called; `mySet`.

Key

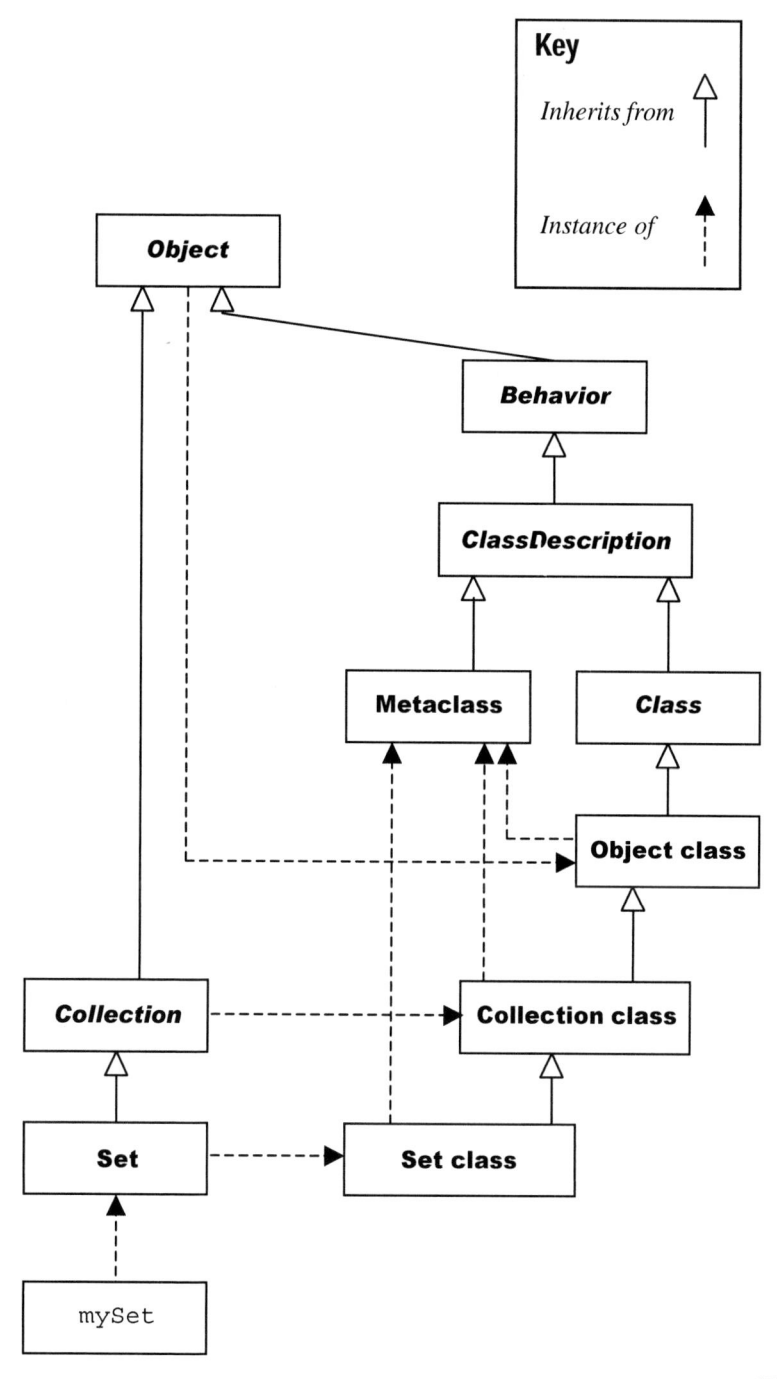

Inherits from △↑

Instance of ▲↑

Methods

Also see:
Class method, Instance method, Messages

When an object receives a message, it has to carry out the associated actions. These actions are defined by the Smalltalk code in the corresponding method. Thus, when an object receives a message, it finds the corresponding method (which has the same name as the message) and executes the code within it.

Methods are used to implement behaviour. They can be instance methods or class methods.

Model View Controller

Also see:
Dependency mechanism, Models

Word processing programs have been around for some time and the basic functions of typing, editing, printing etc. has remained pretty much the same. However, the user interfaces have certainly changed a lot. Some systems even offer a choice of interfaces; eg for expert or for novice use.

The flexibiliy to make changes to an interface, without affecting the underlying program, can only be assured by ensuring there is a clean separation between the parts. The Model-View-Controller (MVC) concept is a way of designing application software so it easier to change some parts without affecting others.

The *Model* in MVC is short for the term domain model, which refers to objects that exist in relation to the underlying problem area that the software is to address. The domain model can be implemented and tested separately from its user interfaces.
The *View* refers to the view the user has of information held in the domain model. It presents the output to the user.
The *Controller* handles input, typically via the keyboard and mouse.

Separating the domain model from the interface allows us to create multiple views of the same underlying data. If this data changes, the different views need to be updated appropriately. The dependency mechanism is used to ensure views stay up-to-date with the domain model. The model informs all its dependent views when any change has occurred.

The following, describes how Smalltalk implements the necessary independence. The state of the objects in the domain model is determined by their attribute values accessed via setter and getter methods. To maintain independence between the user interface and the domain model, we need to ensure that the interface does not need to know the names of the model's setter and getter methods. This is achieved using an object called an *Aspect Adaptor*, which sits between the model and the interface to act as a communication go-between. The *Aspect Adaptor* (an instance of **AspectAdaptor**) handles `value:` messages from the *Controllers* (ie user input) and `value` messages from the *Views*.

Assume we have a **Person** object with instance variable `name`. This variable is accessed via setter method `name: aString` and getter method `name`. An instance of the class **AspectAdaptor** is made a dependent of this **Person** object, and the interface *Controller* and *View* are made dependents of the **AspectAdaptor** object.

The following numbered steps describe the sequence of message-passing events involved when the user enters a new name; `'Peter'`. This change is to be stored by the **Person** object and displayed by the interface.

1. The *Controller* sends a `value: 'Peter'` message to the **AspectAdaptor** object.
2. The **AspectAdaptor** object uses the setter method to pass this on to the **Person** object. ie it sends the message `name: 'Peter'`.
3. The **Person** object stores the value and sends itself a `changed` message.
4. The `changed` message causes an `update: with: from:` message to be sent to the **AspectAdaptor** object.
5. The **AspectAdaptor** object passes an `update: with: from:` message to its dependent *View*.
6. The *View* responds by sending a `value` message to the **AspectAdaptor** object.
7. The **AspectAdaptor** sends a `name` message to the **Person** object to retreive the name value in order to pass it back to the *View* for display.

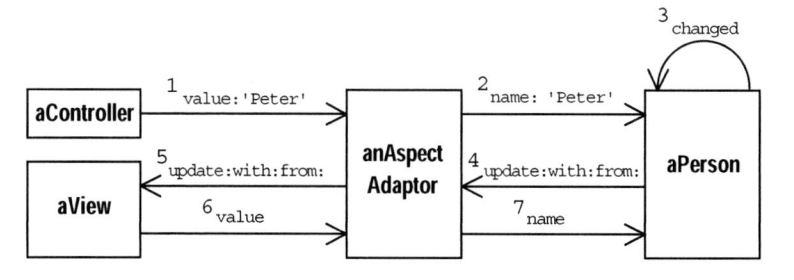

```
                1                          2
                value:'Peter'              name:'Peter'          3 changed
 aController  ───────────────▶  anAspect  ───────────────▶  aPerson
              ◀───────────────   Aspect    ◀───────────────
                5                Adaptor    4
   aView        update:with:from:            update:with:from:
              ◀───────────────            ───────────────▶
                6 value                    7 name
```

109

Models

Also see:
**Dependency mechanism,
Model View Controller**

An application for which software is developed may stay fairly constant with respect to the underlying problems it addresses.

However, its user interface may need to change more frequently. For example, the essence of a word processing application would always need to include facilities to cut, copy and paste text, yet interfaces that are easier to use may be developed, or different interfaces may be required to aid disabled users.

The same application may also feature alternative interfaces for expert and novice users. It therefore makes sense to keep the objects involved in implementing the inner working of an application separate from those comprising the interface.

The objects that implement the underlying problem handling are said to make up the domain model.

The application model comprises a class that provides a connection between the domain model and the user interface.

The application model converts messages from the interface into appropriate messages for the domain objects, and vice versa.

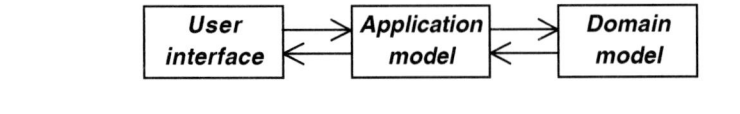

User interface	→ ←	Application model	→ ←	Domain model

nil

Also see:
UndefinedObject

`nil` is a special kind of Smalltalk object. All newly created variables initially point to `nil`, which means that they are unassigned, having no valid value.
`nil` is the sole instance of the class **UndefinedObject**.
It is possible to 'unassign' any variable by assigning `nil` to it.
For example;
    emptyVariable:=nil

The message `isNil` answers `true` if sent to an unassigned variable. Sometimes `nil` is used as the return value on exiting a method, to indicate that the method has not been successful.

Also see:
   Float, Fraction, Integer

Number

The class **Number** is an abstract class that defines the common protocol, inherited by its subclasses.
Instances of the subclasses of **Number** do not have to be created explicitly as they are pre-existing, immutable objects.

Class hierarchy:

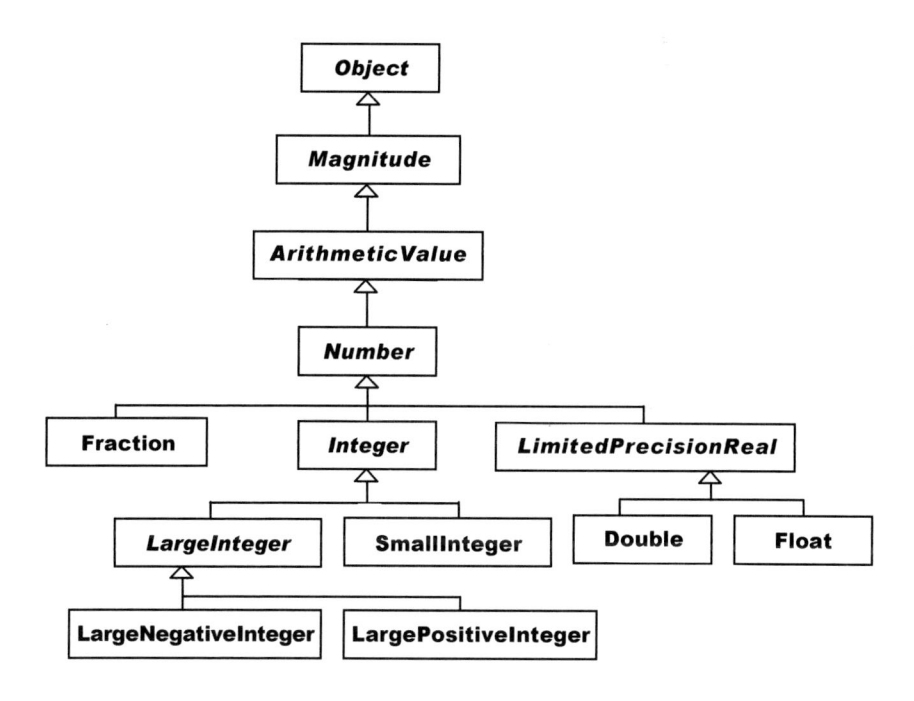

```
                    Object
                      ▲
                   Magnitude
                      ▲
                ArithmeticValue
                      ▲
                    Number
                      ▲
      ┌───────────────┼────────────────┐
   Fraction        Integer      LimitedPrecisionReal
                      ▲                 ▲
             ┌────────┴──────┐    ┌─────┴─────┐
        LargeInteger    SmallInteger  Double    Float
             ▲
   ┌─────────┴──────────┐
LargeNegativeInteger  LargePositiveInteger
```

Number defines the arithmetic protocol that must be implemented by its subclasses. For example, the methods; +, -, * and /.

Number also implements numerical methods that its subclasses can inherit such as;
   `cos, sin, tan, sqrt`

Object

Also see:
Class, Class hierarchy

The **Object** class is the 'mother' of all classes and defines the protocol common to all objects. It is the root class from which all other classes ultimately inherit. As such, there is quite a lot of general class behaviour that is implemented in the **Object** class.

For example, the message `class` is defined by **Object**. When any object is sent this message, it responds with the name of its class.

It is also where the buck stops when it comes to error handling, and it also handles the system dependency mechanism.
It defines the method `doesNotUnderstand:` which provides the default behaviour when a message-send has not been understood. This opens a *Notifier* window, telling the user there has been a problem and from this the user can open a *Debugger* window.
For example, in the *Workspace*, I tried to send a message `jump` to an object that does not have `jump` in its protocol and this *Notifier* window was the result.

Object-oriented programming

Also see:
Abstraction, Encapsulation, Inheritance, Polymorphism, Smalltalk

Smalltalk is an object-oriented programming language and, as such, supports the following characteristics;

- Abstraction
- Encapsulation
- Inheritance
- Polymorphism

Also see:
Attribute, Behaviour

Objects

Objects are the basic building blocks of object-oriented languages such as Smalltalk. They represent data and are classified in types or classes, some of which are built into the language environment. Others can be created by application developers, or obtained from a class library.

For example;

```
42              "is an object of class SamllInteger"
$A              "is an object of class Character; the letter A"
'Eric'          "is an object of class ByteString"
#(1 2 3 4)      "is an object of class Array"
aPerson         "could represent an object created by the
                 programmer, say of class Person"
```

Complex objects can have attributes that describe their characteristics, and behaviour that defines what they do when they receive an instruction in the form of a message from the user or from another object.

Also see:
Collection, Priority queue, Queue, SortedCollection, Stack

OrderedCollection

OrderedCollection is a Smalltalk class. It is a kind of **Collection**.
See *Collection* for class hierarchy.

Objects of any kind can be placed in an instance of **OrderedCollection**.
An instance of **OrderedCollection** can hold any number of objects and will grow or shrink appropriately as elements are added or removed.
The elements do not have to be in any sorted order but are added or removed in a very controlled manner from the front or the back of the collection.
An instance of **OrderedCollection** can contain duplicate elements.

Creation
You can create an instance of **OrderedCollection** by sending a `new` message to the class **OrderedCollection**.

The following statement creates an empty instance of **OrderedCollection**.

```
myOrderedCollection := OrderedCollection new
```

Adding elements
To add elements to an **OrderedCollection** instance, send an `addFrist:` or an `addLast:` message.
`addFirst:` adds an element to the front of the collection and `addLast:` adds to the end.

```
|myOrderedCollection|
myOrderedCollection:= OrderedCollection new.
myOrderedCollection addFirst: 'Eric'.
myOrderedCollection addLast: 'Anita'.
myOrderedCollection addFirst: 'Peter'
```

The above program creates an instance of **OrderedCollection** then adds three elements resulting in `myOrderedCollection` referencing ('Peter' 'Eric' 'Anita').

Retrieval
To retrieve an object from an instance of **OrderedCollection**, you can use `removeFirst` or `removeLast`, as appropriate.

The following program creates an instance of **OrderedCollection**, adds three elements, and then removes the last element.

```
|myOrderedCollection|
myOrderedCollection:= OrderedCollection new.
myOrderedCollection addFirst: 'Eric'.
myOrderedCollection addLast: 'Anita'.
myOrderedCollection addFirst: 'Peter'.
myOrderedCollection removeLast
```

Size
To determine the size of an **OrderedCollection** object, send it the `size` message as follows.

```
myOrderedCollection size
```

Iteration

To iterate over the elements in an instance of **OrderedCollection**, you can use a `do:` message. The following program creates an instance of **OrderedCollection** containing five integer numbers, and then iterates through the contents to calculate their sum and present it as a string.

```
|myOrderedCollection total|
sum := 0.
myOrderedCollection := OrderedCollection new.
myOrderedCollection addFirst: 5; addFirst: 2;
     addFirst: 3; addFirst: 8; addFirst: 6.
myOrderedCollection do: [:element | sum :=
                                    sum + element].
^sum printString
```

Use

An **OrderedCollection** instance is useful for managing data structures such as Queues and Stacks.

Also see:
Abstract method, Inheritance, Methods, Polymorphism

Overriding

When a message is sent to an object, it looks in its class definition for a corresponding method. If the appropriate method cannot be found, it searches in its superclass, and so on, up the class hierarchy until the method is found. Thus, a class inherits methods from its superclasses.

Sometimes, an inherited method is not wanted, because it does not reflect the needs of a subclass. In this situation, the subclass can define a method using the same method name, but with its own required behaviour coded in the implementation. This is called overriding an inherited method.

In situations where there is a method defined in a superclass, but the subclass is to do nothing in response to the corresponding message, the subclass can override the inherited behaviour by implementing its own method that simply does nothing.

115

Polymorphism

Also see:
Method, Object-oriented programming, Overriding

Polymorphism is an important feature of object-oriented languages. It describes the property that allows different objects to respond to the same message, but with their own distinctive behaviour.

For example, the detailed process involved in printing text to a printer is different to that required for printing pictures. A separate method is needed for each. In the following message expressions, `printPicture` is required for **Picture** objects, and `printText` for **TextDocument**.

```
aPicture printPicture
aTextDocument printText
```

Polymorphism allows the same message to be sent to different objects and for them to carry out their own particular methods as a result. So the **Picture** class and the **TextDocument** class could both implement their own methods called `print`.

This makes life simpler because an application that handles objects of both classes could simply send a `print` message to either object type. We could even introduce a new class of objects to be printed and, provided we define an appropriate `print` method, our existing application should work satisfactorily with it, without requiring any alteration.

(My wife and I are polymorphic in taste. Send me a rice pudding and I'll be sick; send the same thing to my wife and she'll salivate!)

Precedence

Also see:
(), Expressions, Messages

Precedence rules determine the order of processing of a Smalltalk expression. The order of evaluation is as follows:

1. Unary messages
2. Binary messages
3. Keyword messages

In the case of equal precedence, processing takes place left to right.

Parentheses can be used to override the normal precedence rules with sub-expressions within the parentheses being evaluated first, working from inner parentheses out.
The expression;
```
9 + 6 negated
```
is evaluated as `9 + (6 negated)`, giving `9 + (-6)`, giving `3`. The unary message `negated` is evaluated before the binary message; `+ 6`.

In the following example, the `raisedTo:aNumber` method answers the receiver raised to the power of the argument, so `2 raisedTo: 2` is equivalent to 2^2.
The message expression:
```
2 raisedTo: 2 + 2
```
is evaluated as `2 raisedTo:(2 + 2)`, giving `2 raisedTo:4`, which answers `16`. The binary sub-expression `2 + 2` is evaluated before the `raisedTo:` keyword message.

Be very careful with message expressions such as;
```
5 + 2 * 3
```
which is evaluated strictly left to right, answering `21`.

Using the normal mathematical precedence of multiply and divide before add and subtract, we would expect the above answer to be `11`. To achieve this result, we would need to place parentheses as follows;
```
5 + (2 * 3)
```

To avoid possible confusion, it is generally clearer to always use parentheses.

Parentheses can be nested and are evaluated from the innermost first.
So;
```
15 + ( 6 *((2 / 2) - 3))
```

evaluates to `15 + (6 * (1 - 3))` which evaluates to;
```
15 + (6 * -2)
```

which evaluates to `15 - 12`, which finally answers `3`.

printString

Also see:
String

The `printString` method answers a string object whose characters are a description of the receiver.
For example;
```
5 printString              "answers '5' "
(7 * 9) printString        "answers '63' "
```

Note that the expression;
```
7 * 9 printString
```

gives an error because the precedence rules dictate that the unary message expression `9 printString` is evaluated first. This answers `'9'`. Then the binary expression `7 * '9'` results in an error because we cannot multiply a number by a string.
The expression;
```
(7 * 9) printString
```

solves the problem by using parentheses to alter the order of precedence.

If you are using LearningWorks™, the result of expressions executed in the *Evaluation Pane* are displayed in the *Display* pane. However, if you are using VisualWorks™ expressions are entered in a *Workspace* window. Output can be directed to another window called *Transcript* by sending appropriate messages to the class **Transcript**.

For example;
```
Transcript show: 'Eric Tatham'
```

will, when evaluated, display the string `'Eric Tatham'` in a *Transcript* window.

For objects that are not already strings, the message `printString` provides a printable textual representation.

118

The expression;
```
    Transcript show: 42 printString
```
or, in LearningWorks™, just;
```
    42 printString
```
displays `'42'`.

The expression;
```
    Date today printString
```
displays `'January 23, 2003'` or whatever today's date is when you execute it.

Some classes define alternative formats.
For example;
```
    Date today shortPrintString
```
answers `'1/23/03'`.

For objects that do not override `printString`, the textual representation returned is a string identifying the class name.

For example;
```
    myCar := Car new.
    myCar printString
```
answers with the string `'Car'`.

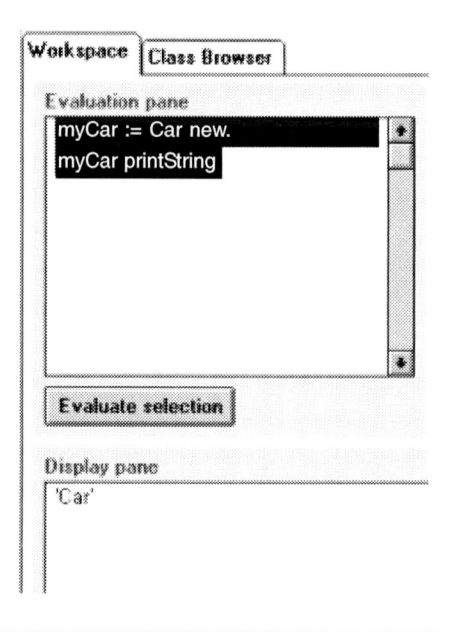

119

Priority queue

Also see:
OrderedCollection, Queue, Stack

A *Priority Queue* is a data structure that is a collection of objects with controlled behaviour, such that new objects are always added to the collection according to some priority criterion, and items to be removed are always taken from the front.

A priority queue could be used for maintaining a list of events to be handled by a computer processor. This creates a computer form of queue jumping in which new events are added to the queue at a position based on their priority rating.

Queue

Also see:
OrderedCollection, Priority queue, Stack

A *Queue* is a collection of elements in which new items are added to the back and elements are always retrieved from the front. This is similar in concept to a queue at a supermarket checkout where new customers join the back of the queue and the first to leave are those at the front.

In computer science, this is behaviour is required frequently. For example, queuing items to be output to a shared printer.

A queue is called a *First In, First Out* (FIFO) structure.

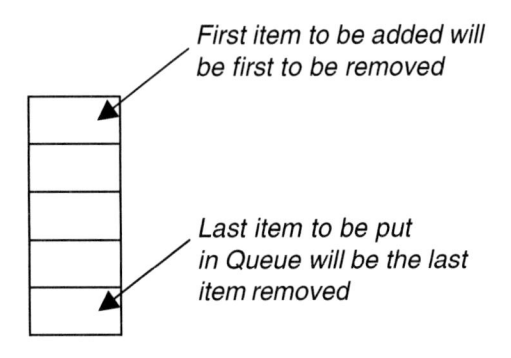

First item to be added will be first to be removed

Last item to be put in Queue will be the last item removed

Queues are easy to implement in Smalltalk using **OrderedCollection**.

Also see:
Number, Streams

Random

An instance of class **Random** generates a stream of pseudo-random numbers between 0.0 and 1.0.
The instance method `next` returns the next number in the stream.

In the following example, a random number between `1` and `6` is generated to simulate the throw of a die.

```
|rand die|
rand := Random new.
die := ((rand next) * 6) + 1.
^ die floor
```

Also see:
Expressions, Messages

Receiver

In a message-sending expression, the object being sent the message is called the receiver.
In the following expression;
    `'eric' asUppercase`
the **String** object `'eric'` is the receiver and `asUppercase` is the message. The answer is `'ERIC'`.

In the message expression;
    `5 + 8`
the **Integer** object `5` is the receiver and `+ 8` the message, where `+` is a binary message selector and `8` is its argument.

Similarly in the expression;
    `age < 17`
the variable `age` is the receiver and `< 17` is the message.

A receiver can be any object or message expression, including a variable reference to an object.

121

Recursion

Also see:
Methods

Recursion occurs when an expression within a method sends a message that causes the same method to be executed again. Of course, this in turn causes the method to call itself again, and again, and again ....

Well, you get the idea!

The following method is recursive because it calls itself.

```
doSomething
    "Illustrative recursive method"

    self doSomething
```

If the `doSomething` method were to be run, it would cause itself to execute again and again in a never-ending recursive loop until the system locks up or crashes.

It is quite easy to do this inadvertently if a method is defined in a superclass and overridden in a subclass. See *Instance creation* for an example.

Recursion can actually be very useful, provided some changing condition is monitored by the method on each iteration and at some stage it causes the recursion to terminate. Searching certain types of data structure is one common use of recursion. However, as I've said, if no termination occurs, it goes on until the execution stack is full and the program will probably just appear to lock up the processing on your machine.

Also see:
  Float, Integer

Rounding

The **Number** class implements a variety of instance methods designed to return a rounded or truncated integer.

The message `floor` answers the integer nearest the receiver toward negative infinity.
```
2.3 floor.         "answers 2"
-2.3 floor.        "answers -3"
2.7 floor.         "answers 2"
-2.7 floor         "answer -3"
```

The message `rounded` answers the integer nearest the receiver.
```
2.3 rounded.       "answers 2"
-2.3 rounded.      "answers -2"
2.7 rounded.       "answers 3"
-2.7 rounded       "answers -3"
```

The message `truncated` answers an integer nearest the receiver toward zero.
```
2.3 truncated.     "answers 2"
-2.3 truncated.    "answers -2"
2.7 truncated.     "answers 2"
-2.7 truncated     "answers -2"
```

The message `ceiling` answers the integer nearest the receiver toward positive infinity.
```
2.3 ceiling.       "answers 3"
-2.3 ceiling.      "answers -2"
2.7 ceiling.       "answers 3"
-2.7 ceiling       "answers -2"
```

123

Scope

Also see:
Global variables, Local variables, Temporary variables, Variables

The scope of a variable determines the regions of program code from which the variable may be used.

The scope of a temporary variable is the statement series in which it is declared. This means that the variable can be used in a statement in the series.

A variable declared within a method comes into existence when the method is run and the declaration executed. It is destroyed when the method ends. The variable is said to be within scope inside the method in which it is declared and out of scope everywhere else.

The scope of a global variable is the entire Smalltalk environment.

The scope of an instance variable is the instance methods of the class in which it is defined, and its subclasses.

The scope of a class variable is the instance and class methods of the class in which it is defined, and its subclasses.

self

Also see:
super, Variables

`self` is a special kind of variable. It is called a pseudo-variable because, like any other variable, it can refer to different objects but, unlike other variables, it cannot be assigned a value using `:=` .

So the attempt to make an assignment, such as; `self := 42` is not allowed.

`self` serves a special purpose. It is used in method code to refer to the receiver of the message that the method implements. The problem that `self` solves by doing this is that a method is part of a class definition so, when its code is written, we do not know the actual object instance to which it might be sent. If we want to refer to that receiver object within the method, we do not know its name, so we call it `self`.

Assume we have a **BankAccount** class with instance variable `balance` to record the balance of an account. The class implements setter and getter methods for `balance` and a further method `sameBalanceAs:` that sets the `balance` of the receiver account to the `balance` of the argument.

Also assume that we have created two instances of **BankAccount**, referenced by `myAccount` and `yourAccount` respectively.

To make the `balance` of `myAccount` the same as the `balance` of `yourAccount`, we would use the expression;

```
myAccount sameBalanceAs: yourAccount
```

or to set the `balance` of `yourAccount` to the same `balance` as `myAccount`;

```
yourAccount sameBalanceAs: myAccount
```

To define the method `sameBalanceAs:` we would use the code;

sameBalanceAs: aBankAccount
"Sets the balance of the receiver to the same value as the balance of the argument aBankAccount. Answers the receiver"

```
self balance: (aBankAccount balance)
```

The expression `(aBankAccount balance)` answers the current balance of the argument represented by `aBankAccount`. This result is then used as the argument to the setter method `balance:`. The `balance:` message must be sent to the receiver of the original `sameBalanceAs:` message. However, when writing the method code we wouldn't have known whether this receiver would be `myAccount`, `yourAccount` or any other specific **BankAccount** instance, so we cannot name it here and refer to it using the name `self`.

Note that, when the method is invoked, the `aBankAccount` parameter will be bound to whatever object is used in the calling argument, so there is no reference problem with this.

125

Set

Also see:
Bag, Collection, Difference, Intersection, Union

Set is a Smalltalk class. It is a subclass of **Collection**.
See *Collection* for class hierarchy.

Objects of any kind can be placed in an instance of **Set** and it can hold any number of objects. It grows and shrinks in size as required.
The elements in a **Set** instance are unordered and not indexed.

Set is very similar to **Bag** but, unlike **Bag**, it cannot contain duplicates.

Creation
You can create an instance of **Set** by sending a `new` message to the class **Set**.

The following statement creates an empty instance of **Set**.

```
mySet := Set new
```

Adding elements
To add elements to a **Set** instance, send an `add:` message.

```
|mySet|
mySet := Set new.
mySet add: 3.
mySet add: 'Eric'
```

The above program creates an instance of **Set** and adds two elements, resulting in `mySet` referencing (3 'Eric').

If we now send `mySet` the message `add: 'Eric'`;
```
mySet add: 'Eric'
```

`mySet` still contains (3 'Eric') because duplicate elements are NOT allowed.

Size
To determine the size of a **Set** object, send it the `size` message as follows.

```
mySet size
```

Iteration
To iterate over the elements in an instance of **Set**, you can use a do: message.

The following program creates an instance of **Set**, putting four integer numbers inside, and then iterating through the contents to calculate their total.

```
|mySet total|
total := 0.
mySet := Set new.
mySet add: 4; add: 6; add: 3; add: 2.
mySet do: [:element | total := total + element].
total printString
```

Use
A **Set** instance is useful for managing a collection that requires no particular ordering, can grow and shrink in size, and cannot contain duplicate elements.

Also see:
   Object-oriented programming   **Smalltalk**

Smalltalk originated from the work of Alan Kay at Xerox Parc in the 1970s. It was one of the first object-oriented languages and is still perhaps the purest in embodying object-oriented concepts. The early work on Smalltalk was closely associated with the ideas that led to the Apple Lisa™ and Macintosh™ interfaces that where the forerunners and inspiration for the interfaces we are familiar with today.
There are a number of Smalltalk environments available including;

VisualWorks   (www.cincom.com)
Dolphin Smalltalk   (www.object-arts.com)
GNU Smalltalk   (www.gnu.org)
Squeak Smalltalk   (www.squeak.org)

The Open University course, M206 Computing: An Object-Oriented Approach, uses LearningWorks™ from Neometron Inc., which was developed based on VisualWorks™.
Smalltalk acts like an interpreted language in that code in a **Workspace** can be executed immediately without a visible compilation process. However, when

methods are written and submitted, they are checked by a compiler and, if free from syntax errors, are compiled to an intermediate form called bytecode. This bytecode is interpreted at run time. The interpreter software changes the bytecode to machine code that can be executed by the computer's processor. This makes execution faster than if the original code text were interpreted.

Sort block

Also see:
Block, SortedCollection

A sort block is a two-argument block used to determine the sorting order for an instance of **SortedCollection**.

It is used as the argument to the `sortBlock:` class method.
For example;

```
mySortedCollection :=
    SortedCollection sortBlock: [:predecessor
        :successor | predecessor > successor]
```

creates an instance of **SortedCollection** with sort order defined by the sort block;

```
[:predecessor :successor | predecessor > successor]
```

and assigns the instance to the variable `mySortedCollection`.

The block arguments `predecessor` and `successor` represent adjacent pairs of objects in the collection, and `predecessor > successor` specifies the sorting criterion. In this case, objects in the collection must be sorted so that, for each adjacent pair of objects, the `predecessor` is greater than the `successor`; ie in reverse numerical or alphabetical order.

(Note that the block arguments can use any variable names and are not restricted to being called `predecessor` and `successor`.)

When a **SortedCollection** is created without specifying a sort block, the default sort block is applied;

```
[:predecessor :successor | predecessor <= successor]
```

which sorts in ascending order.

The following example sorts a collection of words in order of word size and thus answers the **SortedCollection** ('Ian' 'Eric' 'Lynda')

```
|words|
words := SortedCollection sortBlock:
              [:a :b | (a size) <= (b size)].
words add: 'Eric'; add: 'Lynda'; add: 'Ian'.
^words
```

An existing **SortedCollection** can be re-sorted at any time using the `sortBlock:` instance method (as opposed to the class method described above) to the **SortedCollection** instance.

The following expression would reverse the sort order of the previous program, answering the **SortedCollection** ('Lynda' 'Eric' 'Ian').

```
words sortBlock: [:a :b | (a size) >= (b size)].
```

Also see:
  Collection, OrderedCollection,
  Sort block

SortedCollection

SortedCollection is a Smalltalk class. It is a kind of **Collection**.
See *Collection* for class hierarchy.

Objects of any kind can be placed in an instance of **SortedCollection**.
An instance of **SortedCollection** can hold any number of objects and will grow or shrink appropriately as elements are added or removed.
SortedCollection is similar to **OrderedCollection** except that elements are not added to the front or back, but are inserted according to a defined sorting criterion.
An instance of **SortedCollection** can contain duplicate elements.

Creation
You can create an instance of **SortedCollection** by sending a `new` message to **SortedCollection**.

The following statement creates an empty instance of **SortedCollection**.

```
SortedCollection := SortedCollection new
```

Adding elements

To add elements to an instance of **SortedCollection**, send an `add:` message.

```
|mySortedCollection|
mySortedCollection:= SortedCollection new.
mySortedCollection add: 67; add: 23; add: 81;
                                    add: 15.
```

The above program, creates an instance of **SortedCollection** and adds four elements, resulting in `mySortedCollection` containing `(15 23 67 81)` sorted into ascending numerical order.

Size

To determine the number of elements in a **SortedCollection** object, send it the `size` message as follows.

```
mySortedCollection size
```

Iteration

To iterate over the elements in an instance of **SortedCollection**, you can use a `do:` message.
The following program creates an instance of **SortedCollection** containing four integer numbers, and then iterates through the contents to calculate their sum.

```
|mySortedCollection total|
sum := 0.
mySortedCollection:= SortedCollection new.
mySortedCollection add: 67; add: 23; add: 81;
                                    add: 15.
mySortedCollection do: [:element |
                       sum := sum + element].
^sum printString
```

Sort order

To change the sort order to something other than ascending numerical order, send a `sortBlock:` message to **SortedCollection**.

130

The following message creates an instance of **SortedCollection** with the sort order descending numerically.

```
mySortedCollection := SortedCollection
                     sortBlock: [:x :y | x > y].
```

Thus, the following program results in the collection containing (81 67 23 15) sorted into descending numerical order.

```
|mySortedCollection|
mySortedCollection := SortedCollection
                     sortBlock: [:x :y | x > y].
mySortedCollection add: 67; add: 23; add: 81;
                   add: 15.
```

In the block following the `sortBlock:` the variables x and y represent adjacent pairs of objects in the collection. The message expression x > y specifies the sort criterion. Whenever a new element is added to the collection, the first variable; x, points to the new object and the second variable; y, points to an existing object. The sort block is run, iterating through all existing objects, and the new object is added to the collection at the point x > y becomes true.

The default sort order is ascending, so no `sortBlock:` message is needed if this is the required order.

Use

A **SortedCollection** instance is useful for managing lists that can vary in size but whose elements must be kept in sorted order. For example, a list of Customers sorted alphabetically by name.

Stack

Also see:
OrderedCollection, Priority queue, Queue

A *Stack* is a collection of elements in which new items are added to the front and elements to be retrieved are taken from the front. This is similar to stacking plates where the last to be added to the stack is the first to be removed.

This behaviour is required in computing when an object is to be temporarily held while the processor does another job. The object to be held is placed on a stack so it is the first item to be retrieved when the attention of the processor returns.

A stack is called a *First In, Last Out* (FILO) data structure.

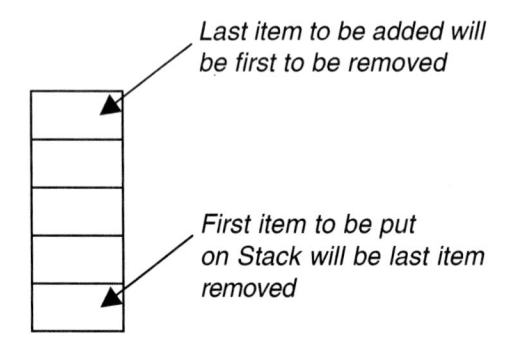

Last item to be added will be first to be removed

First item to be put on Stack will be last item removed

Pop
When an object is removed from the stack, it is said to be popped from the stack.

Push
When an object is added to a stack it is said to be pushed onto the stack.

Stacks fairly straightforward to implement in Smalltalk using **OrderedCollection**.

Also see:
Attribute, Variables

State

The state of an object is defined by the values of its attributes.

For example, if we have a class **Car** with instance variables `make` and `colour`, the state of an instance of **Car**, let's call it `myCar`, is determined by the values of `make` and `colour`.

The following *Inspector* windows show `myCar` in two different states.

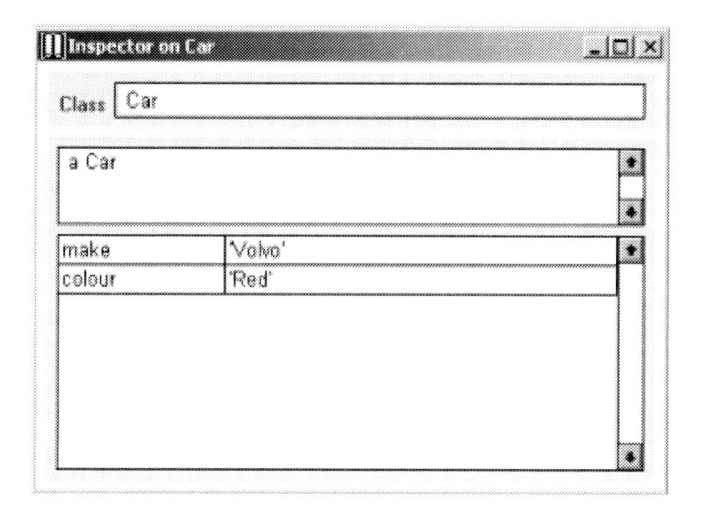

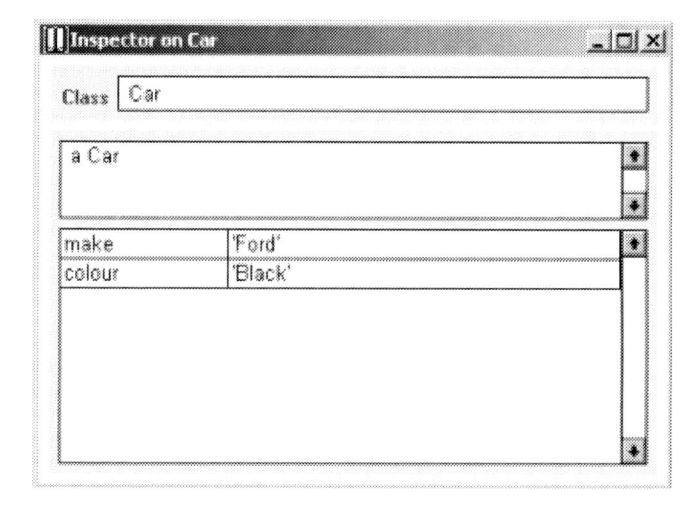

Inspector on Car	
Class	Car
a Car	
make	'Volvo'
colour	'Red'

Inspector on Car	
Class	Car
a Car	
make	'Ford'
colour	'Black'

133

Streams

Also see:
Files, Random

The purpose of **Stream** objects is to support sequential access to collections and files. This is necessary for handling input from the mouse and keyboard, as well as for reading and writing files on disk. It is also useful for accessing internal collections such as strings and arrays.

There are several classes in the **Stream** class hierarchy and these may vary slightly depending on the Smalltalk system you are using. Different subclasses are used for handling collections and files.

Streams provide many messages for manipulating sequenceable collections and allow us to append to them, even when the collection is of fixed size, as in the case of arrays. Streams also allow us to manipulate the object at any given position in the collection.

Two important subclasses are **InternalStream**, which handles collections, and **ExternalStream**, which is designed to deal with files.

InternalStream's subclasses include; **ReadStream**, **WriteStream** and **ReadWriteStream**. These classes allow read and write access to a collection.

To create a stream object, send the required access class an `on:` or a `with:` message.
Alternatively, you can send the collection object a `readStream` or `writeStream` message.

When a stream created with `on:` is written to, it overwrites existing content, whereas a stream created using `with:` is appended at its end.

The statement;
    stream:=ReadStream on:'Eric'

opens a stream on the string `'Eric'`.

134

To write to a stream we can use the messages;
       `nextPut: anObject`   "puts a single object on the stream"
       `nextPutAll: aCollection`   "puts a collection on the stream as individual objects"

Some messages are provided to make it easier to write useful characters to a stream. These include;
       `space`   "writes a space"
       `tab`   "writes a tab"
       `cr`   "writes a carriage return character"

To read from a stream we can use the messages;
       `next`   "answers the next object in the stream, returning `nil` if it is the end of the stream"
       `next: anInteger`   "answers the next specified number of objects in the stream. This will cause an error if we try to go beyond the end of the stream"
       `contents`   "answers the whole contents of the stream"
       `upTo: anObject`   "answers the objects up to, but not including, the first occurrence of the specified object or the end of the stream, depending on which is reached first. The stream read/write position is left pointing to the object following the specified object"
       `upToEnd`   "answers the entire contents of the stream from the current position to the end"
       `atEnd`   "answers `true` if we are the end of the stream, otherwise `false`"

There are also methods for setting the read/write position. These include;
       `position`   "answers the current position in the stream"
       `postion:anInteger`   "sets the current position"
       `reset`   "sets the position to the start of the stream"
       `skip:anInteger`   "skips forward by the specified number of positions"
       `skipSeparators`   "skips forward past certain characters such as; space, carriage return and tab"

In the following statement sequence, the final line answers `'Eric T'` and leaves the position set at position 6. (Remember that the space is a character.)

```
|input|
input:=ReadStream on: 'Eric Tatham'.
input next: 6
```

The following expression will now answer 6;
```
input position
```

and this expression answers `'atham'`;
```
input upToEnd
```

The following program creates a **ReadStream** on the string `'Eric Tatham'` and a **WriteStream** on an empty string for output. It first writes the characters, up to the space (denoted by `$` followed by a space), to the output stream, then writes `' William '`, and finally writes the end of the input stream to the output. Thus, it inserts my middle name between my first and last names.

```
|input output|
input:=ReadStream on:'Eric Tatham'.
output:=WriteStream on: String new.
output nextPutAll: (input upTo:$ ).
output nextPutAll:' William '.
output nextPutAll: (input upToEnd).
^output contents
```

The object returned is the string; `'Eric William Tatham'`.

For discussion of the use of streams with files, see the section on *Files*.

Also see:
ByteString, Character, Collection

String

String is a Smalltalk class. It is a kind of **Collection**.
See *Collection* for class hierarchy.

In principle, it is similar to **Array** except that it can only contain elements that are instances of **Character**. Each element can be indexed using an integer value to denote its position in the string. The index numbering begins at 1.

String is actually an abstract class that is a superclass of **ByteString**. As we cannot create instances of an abstract class, in practice, when we use a string, it is an instance of the **String** subclass called **ByteString**.

An instance of **ByteString** can hold any number of **Character** objects, but its size is defined when it is created and this cannot be changed later.
A **ByteString** object can contain duplicate elements.

Creation
You can create a new instance by sending a `new:` message to **String**.

The following statement creates an empty instance of **ByteString** with space for six characters.

    myString := String new: 6

It is more usual to create an instance of **ByteString** using a literal as follows;

    myString := 'Eric'

using single quotation marks to delimit the string of characters.

An empty string is denoted by two single quotes with no characters between.

    emptyString := ''

This should not be confused with a double quote " which may look the same on the screen.

137

Adding elements
To add elements to a **ByteString** instance, send an `at: put:` message.

```
|myString|
myString := 'Moose'.
myString at: 3 put: $u
```

The above program, creates an instance of **ByteString** containing `'Moose'`; and then replaces the 3rd element with the letter `u`, thus transforming `'Moose'` to `'Mouse'`. (Note that some Smalltalk systems will not replace an element in a string that was created using a literal, as has been done in the above code sample.)

Retrieval
To retrieve the object at a particular index in a string, send the **ByteString** instance an `at:` message. The following statement answers the character at array index 2.

```
myString at: 2
```

Size
To determine the number of characters in a **ByteString** object, send it the `size` message as follows.

```
myString size
```

Other methods
ByteString objects respond to a number of other messages that are specific to them.

```
'Er' , 'ic'
```

uses the message selector `,` to concatenate the string `'Er'` with the string `'ic'`, to answer the string `'Eric'`.

The following expression answers `'rc'`;
```
'Eric' dropVowels
```

and the next answers `'ERIC'`;
```
'Eric' asUppercase
```

138

Pattern matching
You can check whether a string matches a given pattern by sending the pattern the message `match:` with the string as argument.

    `*`   represents any sequence of characters
    `#`   represents any single character
So;
```
'#pen*' match: 'Spendthrift'     "answers true"
'#pen*' match: 'open'            "answers true"
'#pen'  match: 'ripen'           "answers false"
```

We can also search for characters within a string.
The expressions;
```
'The quick brown fox jumps over the lazy dog'
                        includes: $z.
'The quick brown fox jumps over the lazy dog'
                        occurrencesOf: $o
```
answer `true` and 4 respectively.

We can also get a substring.
The expressions;
```
'The quick brown fox jumps over the lazy dog'
                        copyUpTo: $j.
'The quick brown fox jumps over the lazy dog'
                        copyFrom: 11 to:19
```
answer `'The quick brown fox '` and `'brown fox'` respectively.

Also see:
Class, Class hierarchy, Superclass

Subclass

A subclass is a class that is derived from another class. All classes in Smalltalk are ultimately derived from the class **Object**, which is at the top of the class hierarchy. Subclasses are also known as derived classes and they inherit the attributes and behaviour of their superclasses, which they may extend or override.

In the class hierarchy;

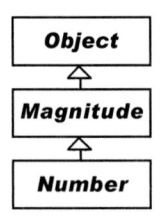

```
   Object
      △
   Magnitude
      △
   Number
```

Number is a subclass of **Magnitude**, which is a subclass of **Object**.
Number is a direct subclass of **Magnitude** but an indirect subclass of **Object**.

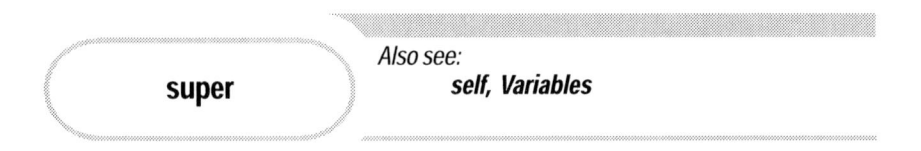

super

Also see:
self, Variables

Like `self`, `super` is also a pseudo-variable. It serves a similar purpose but has a crucial difference. When a message is sent to `super`, it ignores any corresponding method definition in the class of the receiver and the search for the required method starts in the superclass of the class containing the method in which `super` appears.

Consider the following class hierarchy;

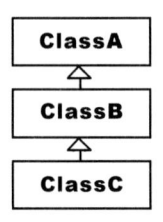

```
   ClassA
      △
   ClassB
      △
   ClassC
```

Assume **ClassA** has an instance method which answers an identifying string;

```
getString
    ^ 'This is Class A'
```

Also assume **ClassB** overrides **ClassA**'s `getString` method;
```
getString
        ^ 'This is Class B'
```

and **ClassC** overrides **ClassB**'s `getString` method;
```
getString
        ^ 'This is Class C'
```

ClassB also has an instance method `test1` that sends a `getString` message to `self`;

```
test1
        ^self getString
```

We can create instances of each class in the *Workspace* as follows;

```
a := ClassA new.
b := ClassB new.
c := ClassC new
```

If we now run;
```
b test1
```

the method code for `test1` substitutes object `b` for `self` and executes;
```
b getString
```

resulting in the answer; `'This is Class B'`

If we run;
```
c test1
```

the search for `test1` begins amongst **ClassC**'s methods. No `test1` is found, so the search continues in the superclass, ie **ClassB**. `test1` is found in **ClassB**'s protocol and its code is run, but `self` is substituted by the original receiver, which was object `c`.
Therefore, the `getString` message is sent to `c`, and the answer is; `'This is Class C'`.

If we now create a **ClassB** method called `test2` that uses `super` instead of `self`;
```
test2
        ^super getString
```

141

When we send the `test2` message to a **ClassB** object;
    b test2

the `getString` definition in the class of the receiver (ie **ClassB**) is ignored, and the method is looked for in the superclass (ie **ClassA**). It is **ClassA**'s `getString` method that is run, giving the answer; `'This is Class A'`.

If we send the `test2` message to a **ClassC** object;
    c test2

because there is no definition of `test2` in **ClassC**'s protocol, it is searched for in the superclass. `test2` is found in **ClassB** so it is this that is run. `super` causes the search for the appropriate `getString` method to begin in the superclass of the class in which the method using `super` is found, which is **ClassA**. So **ClassA**'s `getString` method is run again, answering; `'This is Class A'`.

Superclass

Also see:
Class, Class hierarchy, Superclass

A superclass is a class from which other classes are derived. The derived classes inherit the attributes and behaviour of their superclasses, which they may extend or override.

In this example class hierarchy;

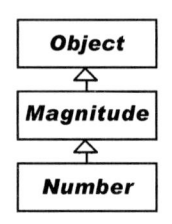

```
Object
  ↑
Magnitude
  ↑
Number
```

Object is a superclass of **Magnitude**, which is a superclass of **Number**. **Object** is a direct superclass of **Magnitude** but an indirect superclass of **Number**.

Also see:
ByteString, Collection, String

Symbol

Symbol is a Smalltalk class. It is a kind of **Collection**.
See *Collection* for class hierarchy.

Symbol has some similarity to **String** but there are some important differences.

An instance of **Symbol** is guaranteed to be unique throughout the system. Hence, an instance of **Symbol** is an immutable object and there cannot be two symbols sharing the same value. It is also fixed in size so cannot grow or shrink. A **Symbol** object is read only and cannot be altered once it has been created, so does not support any methods that would change its value, such as `at:put:`.

A non-empty **Symbol** object can only be created using a literal.

A **Symbol** object is prefixed with a #.
For example;
    #Eric

It is possible to concatenate **Symbol** objects but the result is a **String** object, not a new **Symbol**.

Thus;
      #Er , #ic
answers;
      'Eric'

Uses
Instances of **Symbol** are used to define variable names (identifiers), and method selectors defined for classes.
For example, the class **Person** could include a getter method called `age` to get the person's age. The symbol for the message selector is `#age`.

Symbols can also be used to define unique keys for elements within a **Dictionary** object.

Temporary variable

Also see:
Arguments, Global variable, Local variable, Scope, Variables

Temporary variables are so called because they are discarded after use. They are declared by enclosing them within | symbols before the expression series that uses them.

```
| a b sum |
a := 5.
b := 7.
sum := a + b
```

In the above program, the first line declares the temporary variables; a, b and sum.

Temporary variables can be declared within methods or within blocks. Variables declared in a method are local to that method and, similarly, variables declared in a block are only in scope within the block in which they are declared.

Testing

Also see:
Debugger, Object-oriented programmng

Testing is an important aspect of software development. It is the process by which we try to ensure that software performs in accordance with its design specification.

It is very difficult to fully test complex software as it becomes infeasible to test every possible permutation of data states and execution paths. For this reason testing strategies need to be carefully designed.

Object-oriented development aids testing considerably as software components can often be tested independently of one another.

Black-box and white-box testing

White-box testing (also known as open-box testing) is a software testing strategy in which the internal coding of software units under test can be seen and checked, and appropriate test conditions can be selected on the basis of this knowledge.

In contrast to this, with black-box testing the inner workings of software units are unseen. Testing is based on checking that the inputs and outputs to and from the units perform as required. This has the advantage that the tester does not need to understand the workings of the code.

Object-oriented software units, through the interfaces provided by their methods, are particularly amendable to a black-box approach to testing.

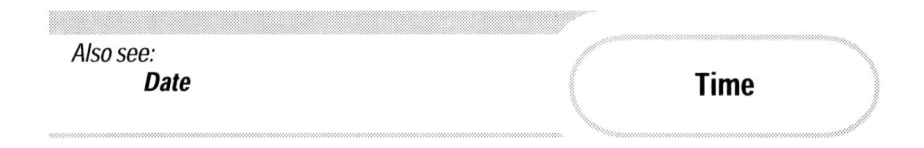

Also see:
   Date   **Time**

Time is a class provided by Smalltalk systems.
Class hierarchy:

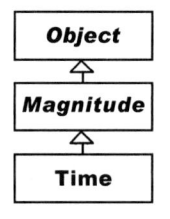

```
    Object
      ▲
   Magnitude
      ▲
     Time
```

An instance of class **Time** represents a particular second in a day. Days start at midnight.

To answer the time now, send the message `now` to class **Time**.

        Time now

To create an instance of **Time**, send the class a message `fromSeconds:` with the number of seconds past midnight as the argument.

The statement;
        breakfastTime := Time fromSeconds: 27000

assigns the **Time** instance `7:30:00 am` to `breakfastTime`.

145

`breakfastTime hours`	"answers the `hour` component of the time represented by the receiver; in this case `7`"
`breakfastTime minutes`	"answers the `minutes` component of the time represented by the receiver; in this case `30`"
`breakfastTime seconds`	"answers the `seconds` component of the time represented by the receiver; in this case `0`"

The method `addTime: timeAmount` can be used to add times. It answers a new **Time** instance that is `timeAmount` after the receiver. `timeAmount` can be an instance of **Date** or **Time**.

Similarly the method `subtractTime: timeAmount` can be used to subtract times. It answers a new **Time** instance that is `timeAmount` before the receiver. `timeAmount` can be an instance of **Date** or **Time**.

Time instances can also be compared;

```
breakfastTime := Time fromSeconds: 27000.
supperTime := Time fromSeconds:72900.

breakfastTime = supperTime         "answers false"
breakfastTime < supperTime         "answers true"
breakfastTime > supperTime         "answers false"
```

Also see:
  Binary message, Keyword message,
  Messages

Unary message

A unary message expression has a single message selector and no argument. For example, in the message expression, to get the current temperature of a **Fridge** object;
    myFridge temperature

`myFridge` is the receiver and is being sent the message `temperature`. The message itself consists of a single message selector (ie `temperature`) and takes no argument, therefore it is a unary message.

The expression;
    2 squared

is also a message expression containing a unary message. In this case, the receiver is the number `2` and is being sent the unary message `squared`.

Also see:
  nil

UndefinedObject

The **UndefinedObject** class has a single instance, which is `nil`.
Class hierarchy:

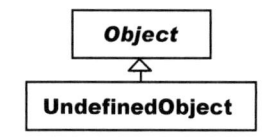

```
      Object
         △
  UndefinedObject
```

A variable references `nil` when it has no meaningful value assigned.

The following expression answers **UndefinedObject**.

    nil class

(Note that `nil` is not equivalent to `0`, which is a **SmallInteger**.)

147

Union

Also see:
Difference, Intersection, Set

The union of two sets is the set that contains all the elements found in either set.

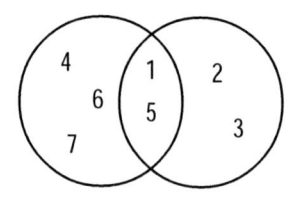

```
    4     1   2
       6
    7     5   3
```

The following method answers the union of two instances of class **Set**.

```
union: aSet to: newSet
"Finds the union of the receiver and aSet and
stores the result in newSet.
Precondition: newSet must be empty
Answers the receiver."

    self do: [:item | newSet add: item].
    aSet do: [:item | newSet add: item]
```

The following program creates three instances of **Set**. setA(1 4 5 6 7) and setB(1 2 3 5) are *unioned* to give the result in setC(1 2 3 4 5 6 7).

```
|setA setB setC|
setA := Set new.
setB := Set new.
setC := Set new.
setA add: 1; add: 4; add: 5; add: 6; add: 7.
setB add: 1; add: 2; add: 3; add: 5.
setA union: setB to: setC
```

The union of two sets is the set that contains all the elements found in either set.

(Note that, if you wish to try this, it is safer to make it an instance method of your own subclass of **Set**, rather than modify the protocol of **Set**.)

148

Also see:
**Class/Instance variable, Scope,
Local/Temporary/Global variable**

Variables

A variable is a name used to reference an object. It provides a way for us to keep track of objects, and as an identifier for sending messages.

There are rules for naming variables. Variable names must start with a letter followed by any alpha-numeric characters. By convention, most variables start with a lowercase letter.

It is helpful to understanding what variables represent if they are given meaningful names. For example, a variable called `age` would be expected to refer to a number representing an age

It is often useful to use more than one word to make the use of a variable absolutely clear. As spaces are not allowed, it is usual to show the start of each new word with an uppercase letter.
For example;
`aBankAccount, ageNextBirthday, vehicleRegistration`

A variable must be declared before use. However, in Smalltalk, unlike many other programming languages, the class of object referred to by a variable is not fixed on declaration. Nevertheless, it is essential that the use of a particular variable remains consistent throughout a program.

A variable can refer to an object of any class and can be bound to the object to which it refers by using an assignment statement.

When first declared, an uninitialised variable refers to `nil`. Therefore, the decaration; `|myName|` results in;

$$\text{myName} \dashrightarrow \boxed{\text{nil}}$$

After assignment, such as;
    `myName := 'Eric'`

the variable references an object.

$$\text{myName} \dashrightarrow \boxed{\text{'Eric'}}$$

149

Variables can be;
- Instance variables
- Class variables
- Class instance variables
- Parameters
- Temporary variables
- Global variables

Workspace

Also see:
Class browser, Debugger, Inspector

A *Workspace* object is a window, which forms part of the Smalltalk environment and in which statements can be evaluated. This illustration shows a LearningWorks™ *Workspace*.

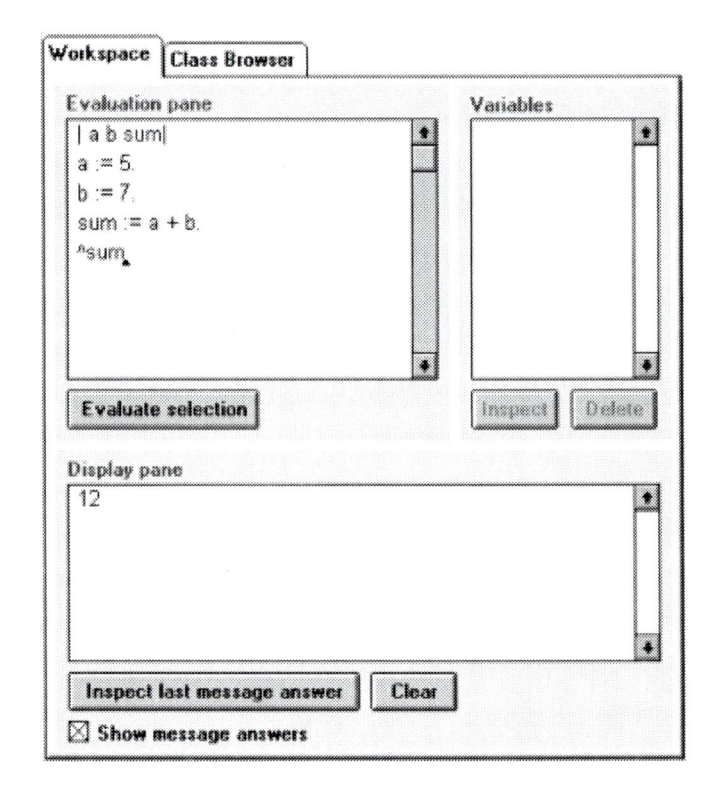

```
| a b sum |
a := 5.
b := 7.
sum := a + b.
^sum
```

150

Index

\# ... 1, 28, 143
$ ... 1, 40
. ... 1
: ... 2
; ... 2
:= ... 2, 30
^ ... 3, 24
, ... 4, 50, 138
+ ... 4, 27
- ... 5, 27
* ... 5, 27
/ ... 6, 27
** ... 6, 27
// ... 7, 27
\\ ... 7, 27
& ... 8, 101
| ... 9, 101
== ... 11, 99
~~ ... 12, 99
= ... 12, 99
~= ... 13, 99
< ... 14, 99
<= ... 14, 99
> ... 15, 99
>= ... 15, 99
@ ... 16
-> ... 16, 31
() ... 17, 116
[] ... 18
abstract class ... 19
abstraction ... 22, 112
accessor method ... 23
add: ... 32, 67, 126, 129
addDays: ... 54
addDependent: ...61
addFirst: ... 114
addLast: ... 114
addSharedPool: ... 81
addTime: ... 146
and: ... 9, 101
answer ... 3, 24
anthropomorphism ... 25
appendStream ... 76
application model ... 110
arguments ... 25
arithmetic operators ... 27
ArithmeticValue ... 111
Array ... 27, 48, 97
ArrayedCollection ... 48
asArray ... 53
asBag ... 53
asCharacter ... 40
asDays ... 54
asFilename ... 76
asFloat ... 52
asInteger ... 52
asLowercase ... 40
asNumber ... 53, 67
asOrderedCollection ... 53
AspectAdaptor ... 109
asRational ... 53
asSet ... 53
assignment ... 2, 30
Association ... 16, 30, 67
asSortedCollection ... 53
asUppercase ... 40, 138
at: ... 28, 67, 138
at:put: ... 28, 67, 80, 138
atEnd ... 135
attribute ... 32
Bag ... 32, 48
Behavior ... 33, 106
behaviour ... 33
between:and: ... 101
binary message ... 34
black-box testing ... 144

151

block ... 18, 35
BlockClosure ... 18, 35
Boolean ... 36
boolean condition block ... 37
BOSS ... 38
bytecode ... 38
ByteString ... 39, 48, 137
ByteSymbol ... 48
cascaded message ... 2
ceiling .. 123
changed ... 62
changed: ... 62
changed:with: ... 62
Character ... 40, 97
CharacterArray ... 48
class ... 41, 105
Class ... 41, 80
class browser ... 42
class hierarchy ... 42
class instance variable ... 43
class library ... 45
class method ... 46
class variable ... 46
ClassDescription ... 106
close ... 77
Collection ... 48
comment ... 49
compiled language ... 38, 50, 90
concatenate ... 4, 50
concatenate: ... 50
concrete class ... 19
conditional expressions ... 51
confirm: ... 65
constant ... 52
contents ... 135
conversion ... 52
copyFrom: ... 139
copyUpTo: ... 139
cos ... 111
cr ... 135
Date ... 53
dateOfMonth ... 54

day ... 54
debugger ... 55
dependency mechanism ... 61, 108
DependentFields ... 63
dependents ... 63
derived class ... 139
Dialog ... 64
Dictionary ... 31, 48, 67
difference ... 70
directory ... 76
direct subclass ...140
direct superclass ... 142
display pane ... 118
do: ... 29, 33, 69, 94, 115, 127, 129
doesNotUnderstand: ... 112
domain model ... 110
Double ... 111
dropVowels ... 138
encapsulation ... 71, 112
equality ... 12
equality vs identity ... 100
errors ... 72
evaluation panel ... 118
expressions ... 74
ExternalStream ... 134
False ... 36
FATFilename ... 76
Filename ... 76
files ... 76
Float ... 78, 96
floor ... 123
Fraction ... 78, 97
fromSeconds: ... 145
garbage collection ... 78
getter method ... 23
global variable ... 79
greater than ... 15, 99
greater than or equal to ... 15, 99
halt ... 55
halt: ... 55
head ... 76
hours ... 146

152

identifier ... 149
identity ... 11
ifFalse: ... 51
ifFalse:ifTrue: ... 51
ifTrue: ... 51
ifTrue:ifFalse: ... 51
immutable object ... 40, 111, 143
includes: ... 139
indirect subclass ... 140
indirect superclass ... 142
inequality ... 13
inheritance ... 81, 112
initialize ... 86
inspect ... 82
inspector ... 82
instance creation ... 83
instance method ... 88
instance variable ... 89
instanceVariableNames: ... 45
Integer ... 90, 96
InternalStream ... 134
interpreted language ... 38, 50, 90
intersection ... 91
isDigit ... 40
isEmpty ... 24
isInteger ... 101
isLowercase ... 40
isNil ... 24, 110
isString ... 101
isUppercase ... 40
isVowel ... 40
iteration ... 92
key ... 31, 67
key:value: ... 31, 67
keysAndValuesDo: ... 70
keyword message ... 95
LargeInteger ... 111
LargeNegativeInteger ... 90
LargePositiveInteger ... 90
leapYear ... 46
leapYear: ... 46
LearningWorks ... 127

less than ... 14, 99
less than or equal to ... 14, 99
LimitedPrecisionReal ... 111
literals ... 96
local variable ... 98
logical error ... 73
logical operators ... 99
machine code ... 39, 50
Magnitude ... 99, 102
match: ... 139
max: ... 101
messages ... 102
Metaclass ... 105
methods ... 108
min: ... 101
minutes ... 146
Model ... 63
model view controller ... 108
models ... 110
monthName ... 54
named: ... 76
negated ... 117
new ... 31, 32, 46, 67, 83, 114, 126, 129
new: ... 28, 83, 137
newDay:
    monthNumber:year: ... 54
next ... 121, 135
next: ... 135
nextPut: ... 135
nextPutAll: ... 77, 135
nil ... 110, 147
notifier ... 55
now ... 145
Number ... 96, 111, 123
Object ... 42, 112
object oriented programming ... 112
objects ... 113
occurrencesOf: ... 139
on: ... 134
or: ... 10, 101
OrderedCollection ... 48, 113, 120, 132
overriding ... 22, 115

153

parameter ... 26
pattern matching ... 139
`plus:` ... 5
Point ... 16
polymorphism ... 112, 116
pool dictionary ... 79
PoolDictionary ... 48, 80
pop ... 132
`position` ... 135
`position:` ... 135
precedence ... 17, 116
precondition ... 26
`printString` ... 118
priority queue ... 120
protocol ... 103
push ... 132
queue ... 120
`raisedTo:` ... 117
Random ... 121
`readStream` ... 76
ReadStream ... 134
`readWriteStream` ... 76
ReadWriteStream ... 134
receiver ... 121
recursion ... 122
`reject:` ... 95
`removeDependent:` ... 63
`removeFirst` ... 114
`removeKey:` ... 69
`removeLast` ... 114
`request:` ... 66
`request:initialAnswer:` ... 66
`request:`
　`initialAnswer:`
　`onCancel:` ... 66
reset ... 135
rounded ... 123
rounding ... 123
sameness ... 11
scope ... 124
seconds ... 146
`select:` ... 94

`self` ... 124
semantic error ... 73
separator ... 1
SequenceableCollection ... 48
Set ... 48, 70, 91, 126, 148
setter method ... 23
`show:` ... 118
sin ... 111
size ... 29, 33, 114, 126, 129, 138
`skip:` ... 135
`skipSeparators` ... 135
SmallInteger ... 90
Smalltalk ... 127
sort block ... 128
`sortBlock:` ... 128, 129
SortedCollection ... 48, 128, 129
space ... 135
sqrt ... 111
`squared` ... 147
stack ... 132
state ... 133
Stream ... 134
streams ... 134
String ... 48, 97, 137
subclass ... 139
`subclass:`
　`instanceVariableNames:`
　`classVariableNames:`
　`poolDictionaries:` ... 41, 81
`subclassResponsibility` ... 22
`subtractTime:` ... 146
super ... 140
superclass ... 106, 142
Symbol ... 48, 97, 143
syntax error ... 73
tab ... 135
`tail` ... 76
tan ... 111
temporary variable ... 144
testing ... 144
Time ... 145
`timesRepeat:` ... 92

154

```
to:do: ... 93
today ... 54
Transcript ... 118
True ... 36
truncated ... 123
unary message ... 147
UndefinedObject ... 110, 147
union ... 148
update:with:from: ... 62
upTo: ... 135
upToEnd ... 135
user interface ... 110
value ... 31, 35, 67
value: ... 35
variables ... 149
version ... 80
virtual machine ... 39
VisualWorks ... 127
warn: ... 64
weekday ... 54
whileFalse: ... 37, 93
whileTrue: ... 37, 92
white-box testing ... 144
with: ... 134
withCRs ... 64
workspace ... 150
writeStream ... 76
WriteStream ... 134
year ... 54
```